# Samuel Gompers

# PRAEGER PATHFINDER BIOGRAPHIES

# Samuel Gompers

## LEADER OF AMERICAN LABOR

### WILL CHASAN

PRAEGER PUBLISHERS
New York · Washington · London

PRAEGER PUBLISHERS
111 Fourth Avenue, New York, N. Y. 10003, U.S.A.
5, Cromwell Place, London S.W.7, England

Published in the United States of America in 1971
by Praeger Publishers, Inc.

Library of Congress Catalog Card Number: 70–86511

Printed in the United States of America

# Contents

5

6                                              *Contents*

# List of Illustrations

7

# Samuel Gompers

"Some men and women, indeed, there are who can live on smiles and the word 'yes' forever. For others . . . some austerity and wintry negativity, some roughness, danger, stringency, and effort, some no! no! must be mixed in to produce the sense of an existence with character and texture and power. The range of individual difference in this respect is enormous; but whatever the mixture of yesses and noes may be, the person is infallibly aware when he has struck it in the right proportion for him. 'This,' he feels, 'is my proper vocation . . . the life for me to live. Here I find the degree of equilibrium, safety, calm, and leisure which I need, or here I find the challenge, passion, fight, and hardship without which my soul's energy expires.' "

—William James

". . . the task of democracy is to relieve mass misery and yet preserve the freedom of the individual."

—Alfred North Whitehead

# I

# *A Prologue*

The *City of London,* described by one of its passengers as an "old tub," sailed out of Chadwick Basin, England, bound for New York, on June 10, 1863. It was to be a trying but uneventful voyage.

The only memorable incident, one gathers from the available record, was the celebration that the captain arranged on July 4. The little sailing ship was then in mid-Atlantic. The captain wanted, no doubt, to divert his passengers. Mainly immigrants, they had been huddled in their cramped quarters, jostled by their bedding, pots, and provisions, for twenty-four days, and most of them were thoroughly seasick. Fireworks were broken out by the crew. A small band was somehow improvised. Forgetting their wretchedness, which must have been extreme, the passengers danced on the lurching deck.

In an important sense, they had reason to dance, or so they thought. New York, though still weeks away, represented a glowing prospect. "To the west, to the west, to the land of the free," went a song popular among emigrants of the time.

Where the mighty Missouri rolls down to the sea,
Where a man is a man if he's willing to toil,
Where the humblest may gather the fruits of the soil.

The song, which promised only that much could be gained by
hard work, had brought the family of Andrew Carnegie, who
was to become a great steelmaker, to this country; its promise
was to lure more than 24 million Europeans in the years
between 1860 and 1920. On board the *City of London* were a
handful of the 176,282 who were to face the trials of the voyage
to the United States, so savagely disunited, in 1863.

One of them was an interesting-looking boy named Samuel
Gompers. He was neither handsome nor tall. But he was thick-
chested, he had a large head, crowned by a mass of dark, wavy
hair, and the line of his jaw hinted at a resolute character. Sam,
as nearly everyone called him, then and throughout his life,
had been born in London's East End on January 27, 1850. He
was not yet thirteen and a half years old. Years later, it would
be said that his head was "Napoleonic" and that his eyes were
those of a man "who saw great visions." But it would be fanci-
ful to suggest that one could read the boy's future in his face.

Even in photographs taken of him after he had grown to man-
hood, when a luxuriant, black handlebar mustache would add a
picturesque quality to his face, there would be no real clue to his
future: He could be a poet or a river-barge fighter, perhaps a
frontier adventurer. Elements of all three, in fact, were to come
together in him in a strange blend that journalists would refer to
as "magnetism," "a dramatic personality that grips and holds
you," "the physical spell of a personal leader." That kind of
personality is rarer than one would suppose in our age of artful
publicity and "image-making." It would enable him, on one
occasion, to reach out calmly and take a gun from the hand
of a man threatening to shoot him; on another, to draw an
audience away from the great actress Ethel Barrymore, in an
Indiana town; and to command the absolute loyalty of the men
around him.

Sam was never to grow beyond five feet, four inches in height, and one of his close friends has told us that his lack of size embarrassed him, but he was to become a towering figure in American life. He would be the leader, in 1886, in founding the American Federation of Labor (AFL), the first organization of its kind to succeed in this country, and, as strategist, spokesman, and philosopher, he would preside over its destiny for nearly forty years. Its policies would be referred to as "Gomperism," and posters heralding his arrival in a town would describe him as "Labor's Foremost Champion." His associates, stiffly independent men, would refer to him as "the Chief."

"I always remained a little awed by him," one of them would write. "Most of us were. He had that effect."

Sam was also to be a center of controversy, often violent and sometimes affecting the course of the nation. In the White House one day, Theodore Roosevelt, the "Rough Rider," a bellicose man, would seek to close a dispute with him abruptly by saying, "But I am President of the United States," and he, respectful but unyielding, would reply, "That is so, Mr. President. But I am President of the American Federation of Labor. I shall protect the interests of the workers, be the consequences what they may." Where the interests of workers, as he saw them, or the liberties of anyone, were involved, he was to be a most stubborn man. "Mr. Gompers," an Attorney General of the United States would say, "I regard you as a spokesman for the underdog of the world."

His career was to keep some Americans in an almost constant state of wrath. Conservatives were to rail at him as a "demagogue" and a "dangerous man." One of them, a judge, would denounce him as the leader of a "seditious rabble" out to "unlaw" the country. Yet, he would seem intolerably conservative to some people. Radicals, whose efforts to capture the American labor movement he would defeat time and again, were to call him a "labor faker," a "greasy tool of Wall Street." "Life has never been tame for me," he would muse in his autobiography, *Seventy Years of Life and Labor*. But, by then, the movement he led, scattered and feeble when he had come on the scene, would be the most powerful of its kind in the world, and it would have caused major changes in American life. By then, too, President Woodrow Wilson would have hailed his "patriotic courage, his large vision, and his statesman-like sense of what has to be done."

"All men and women who work with their hands or heads owe much to Samuel Gompers," it would be said. "He brought to them the right to respect themselves as producers of wealth instead of being merely peons in the service of wealth."

The boy, of course, could have had no notion of what lay before him. Ideas of the labor movement, if they existed in his head, must have been vague. The movement itself was still vague. If he had any dreams of glory, they probably revolved around the theater. In London, his paternal grandfather, Samuel, a scholarly-looking antique dealer, had introduced him to it. He had gone to the theater every time he could scrape a "few pennies" together. Along with opera, it was to hold a lifelong fascination for him.

Now, he was traveling to New York with his Dutch-born Jewish parents, Solomon and Sara Gompers, and his four younger brothers and sister, in the hope that life would be better for them there. The Gompers family, a large one, had a certain luster. Originally, its name had been Gomperz. It could trace its ancestry back to a Dr. Emric Gomperz who had taught Moses Mendelssohn, the great eighteenth-century philosopher, and to others who had gained distinction or wealth. But most of the Gomperses were poor. It was a time when most people were poor. Sam's father, a cigarmaker, had found it impossible to support the family in London.

Sam, shortly after his tenth birthday, had been taken out of the Jewish Free School, which he had entered at the age of six, and apprenticed to a shoemaker. It had not struck him as especially strange or unjust. In the Spitalfields section of the East End, where the Gomperses had lived in a two-room flat on Fort Street, many boys of his age worked. As he had reason to know, worse fates were possible. Among the Gomperses' neighbors were many descendants of the Huguenots who had fled persecution in France. Their skills as weavers had made Spitalfields famous for its silks. Then, suddenly, new machines had displaced hand skills, and many of the weavers had found themselves jobless. One of Sam's "most vivid early recollections" was of the despairing cries of these men clustered in the narrow streets: Their wives and children wanted bread, and they had no work to do. His wages in the shoemaking shop had been only three pence a week; the noise had grated on him. He had shifted his apprenticeship to his father's trade. He had found his new employment, in a factory on Bishopsgate Street owned by a man named David Schwab, more congenial. He would remember Schwab as a "most eccentric individual" who lived above his factory and who frequently came darting down the steps in his nightdress or underwear to spray his workers with orders and rebukes. It was difficult for the boy not to find some humor in the scene.

Cigar factories in those days, in London and elsewhere, often resembled informal study groups. Work was done by hand; there were no machine noises to shred the silence. The men, who sat at long tables as they worked the velvety tobacco leaves into shape, took turns at reading aloud from newspapers and classics. They sang when the spirit moved them. There were lengthy and sometimes heated discussions. It was probably in such discussions at Schwab's that Sam had learned of English workers' sympathy with the Union in the Civil War. English textile workers had lost their jobs when the Union's blockade of Southern ports cut off supplies of cotton. Yet they remained stanchly opposed to slavery. "Slave Ship," a song that told of the horrors of the slave trade, was popular among English workers, and Sam had learned to sing it. He sang it, he later said, "with a fervor" in which all his feelings "throbbed."

He had been paid one shilling, that is, twelve cents, a week during his first year at Schwab's and twice that amount in the second. But his earnings had not added enough to the family purse to enable his father to feed eight mouths. In the United States at the time, wages averaged less than $6 a week. Average annual earnings for an American worker were calculated at $297. These were hardly princely sums. "If I am less troubled concerning the slavery prevalent in Charleston and New Orleans," Horace Greeley, the editor of the New York *Tribune*, had written to an abolitionist friend earlier, "it is because I see so much slavery in New York, which appears to claim my first efforts." Nevertheless, conditions were worse in London and elsewhere in Europe, and there had seemed little hope to the Gomperses that life would yield to their efforts at self-betterment. Sam's parents, after much discussion, had reached the decision that was now taking them westward across the Atlantic.

The two-room flat they had occupied in London must have seemed spacious in retrospect to Sam and his brothers as they chafed under the confinement of the ship. They played with tops. They amused themselves, as best they could, with games. The celebration on July 4 came as a welcome break in their not very amusing amusements. Besides the fireworks and the music, there was a fair of sorts. It contained, Sam solemnly reported, "a marvelous deer with eight legs and two heads." But what impressed him most was the salute to the Stars and Stripes with which the festivities closed. Possibly, the boy sensed that a symbolic transfer of loyalties was involved in the act. In any event, there was to be a time when he would see the American flag "under foreign skies, from the ramparts of a great world war," and think, "America is more than a name, America is an ideal."

However, as the ship sailed slowly toward New York, at the mercy of the winds, its passengers still struggling with their unruly insides, there was little in that city to suggest an ideal of any kind. On March 3, Congress had passed the Conscription

Act to help fill the Union's manpower needs. The Copperheads, who were Northern supporters of the South, were using it to foment discontent in a population already war-weary. New York was one of their strongholds. On July 4, when many of the passengers on the *City of London* were saluting the American flag for the first time, New York Governor Horatio Seymour, an antiwar Democrat, was telling an audience at the Academy of Music that the government was on the "very verge of destruction." It was, he said, "seizing our persons, infringing upon our rights, insulting our homes. . . . Remember this," he added ominously, "the bloody, treasonable, and revolutionary doctrine of public necessity can be proclaimed by a mob as well as by a government." The city was being flooded with such propaganda.

The draft began in New York on Saturday, July 11. Perhaps it was only coincidence that Governor Seymour had left two days earlier for a holiday at a New Jersey seashore resort. On Monday, mobs began forming in the city. They threw up barricades at various points. Armed with guns, iron bars, staves, and other weapons, they rampaged through the city for days. They burned buildings, tore up railroad tracks, pillaged stores, murdered, or brutally beat, any Negroes they could find, and fought pitched battles with the police. "To hell with the draft and the war!" they chanted. "Tell old Abe Lincoln to come to New York!"

The riots were finally quelled on July 16 when five regiments of New York troops, released by the Army of the Potomac, entered the city. But New York was still simmering on Wednesday, July 29, when the *City of London* tied up at the lower end of Manhattan at what was then known as Castle Garden. The Gompers family was made immediately aware of the city's mood. Sam's father shook hands with a Negro who had been helpful to the family during the voyage. A crowd crystallized around them. There were ugly mutterings and threats of hanging Mr. Gompers and the Negro to the nearest lamppost.

After voyaging for fifty days "to the west, to the west, to the land of the free," the Gomperses had arrived. The occasion, so long awaited, must have been at least mildly dismaying. Their new land, they would soon learn, held other dismaying experiences for them.

# 2

# *The Wilderness of Untried Things*

Thomas Jefferson, author of the Declaration of Independence
and third President of the United States, never saw a town
until he was eighteen. He thought that, if God had a "chosen
people," they were the farmers. He regarded city life as cor-
rupting. But the New York in which the Gomperses landed
would probably have been beyond his imagining.

In 1826, when Jefferson died amid the pastoral splendors of
his estate at Monticello, the combined population of the
country's five largest cities, including New York, was less than
a half-million. In 1863, the population of New York alone,
swollen by immigration, exceeded a million. The city had done
little to accommodate its newcomers. Most of the immigrant
poor, mainly Irish, English, Dutch, and German, crammed themselves into the tenements of the lower East Side, which was then
rapidly becoming the most congested slum in the Western
world. An investigator, some years later, was shocked to find a
"family" of mother and father, twelve children, and six boarders
living in two rooms. On their first day in New York, the eight

members of the Gompers family, sharing a wagon with their possessions, rattled over the city's cobblestone streets into this neighborhood. Their first home consisted of four rooms. Only one room had windows. They had to go out into the backyard for water. Toilet facilities, too, were in the backyard. "Conveniences that make water easily usable in the families of the poor," Sam would reflect years later, "have a beneficent value that few can appreciate who have not lived through the privations and hardships of those old days." Nevertheless, after their two-room flat in London, their new home represented progress.

Sam, as he recorded, was then exactly thirteen years, six months, and two days old. He had been a wage-earner for more than three years. His father began to make cigars at home; the boy, resuming his apprenticeship, worked with him. He was not altogether happy in his new environment. The summer heat, far worse than in London, filled their little flat. The screams of animals in a nearby slaughterhouse were unsettling, and the slaughterhouse stench clogged the air. He had always found his mother's Dutch cooking "marvelously delicious," but now, when she served meat, he could not get it down. The city, it was said, had more than 4,000 saloons. In Sam's neighborhood, they were everywhere. Behind the Gomperses' tenement, a brewery was in almost continuous operation, and the boy watched it at times, in fascination, from the tenement's back door. The brewery workers seemed never to go home. Frequently, it appeared to him that they drooped with fatigue. Like the Spitalfields weavers, the brewery workers lodged in his mind.

In London, he had enjoyed exploring the streets. He was sturdy, unafraid, and adventurous. The New York he came to know would startle a voyager from the present even more than it would have startled Jefferson. Open country began less than a mile north of what is now Times Square. There were no tall buildings. The masts of sailing ships in the harbor jutted up past the roof tops. Public transportation, such as it was, consisted of horse-drawn streetcars. On Broadway, or on Fifth Avenue, where Sam sometimes ventured, thousands of livery carriages rolled by with fashionably dressed men and women. One could perhaps see J. Pierpont Morgan, a rising young financier who, with a partner, had just made $160,000 in gold speculation, or Cornelius Vanderbilt, a former ferryman, tough and piratical, who was amassing a great fortune by manipulating shipping and railroad stocks. "Law?" Vanderbilt was quoted as saying. "What do I care about the law? Hain't I got the power?" His arrogance was shared by many of the new financial and industrial barons who were to be Sam's antagonists.

The country's four leading industries were still flour and meal, cotton goods, lumber, and boots and shoes, but the industrial revolution, nourished by the needs of the Civil War, was gaining momentum. The United States, as we know it today, was in the making. The daily parade of carriages on New York's main thoroughfares reflected the fact that it had become the country's financial capital. One could observe in it all the contrasts of poverty and wealth that were to produce turbulent and often bloody class antagonisms. There were "slums crowding the marble palaces of the rich," Lord Bryce wrote in his classic study *American Commonwealth*. Sam would soon be talking bitterly about the "injustices that society meted out to wage-earners."

For a time, however, his chief interest was the Arion Base Ball and Social Club. He organized it when he was fourteen, with some of his friends, and he was elected its president. One wonders how they played baseball, which was then very new, and what they used for equipment. In any event, neither that game nor others seem to have interested them greatly. All of them were immigrants or the sons of immigrants. Herman Melville, the author of *Moby Dick*, had probably expressed their mood when he wrote: "We are the pioneers of the world; the advance guard, sent on through the wilderness of untried things, to break a path in the New World that is ours." They, too, were

pioneers; New York was their wilderness; time was too precious
to be squandered on games. Their interests turned to debates,
mock trials, and other such improving activities. Their little
group, they decided, needed a more appropriate name. It became the Rising Star Social and Debating Club.

The club widened Sam's world considerably. The opportunity
to explore and express his thoughts, and to test them against
criticism, had previously been denied to him. He found that
he enjoyed public speaking. A resonant baritone voice, which
seemed to well up effortlessly from his deep chest, and a sense of
theater, acquired as a boy in London, no doubt contributed to
his pleasure. The debates, in which he excelled, aroused his
mind. "Mental hunger," he discovered, could be "just as painful
as physical hunger."

He began spending evenings and Saturdays at Cooper Union,
then an extraordinary influence in New York life. It had been
established in the late 1850's by Peter Cooper, a philanthropic
inventor and iron manufacturer, for the "advancement of science and the arts," and young East Siders, eager for knowledge,
flocked to it. Cooper had earned fame for having designed and
built the country's first steam locomotive, popularly known as
the *Tom Thumb*, for the Baltimore and Ohio Railroad; it had
convinced the railroad of its superiority over horses by speeding
thirteen miles an hour. But Cooper Union was to be recognized as his greater achievement. It had become a center of
liberal and radical thought, and its Saturday evening lectures
regularly attracted two or three thousand people. Sam, who, in
his own words, was "fairly quivering" in his "intense desire to
know," attended them religiously. He was to attend lectures
and courses at Cooper Union, on and off, for some twenty years.
He made friends there with Peter J. McGuire, an ardent and
idealistic young Irishman, and others with whom he was to be
associated in labor's struggles.

The Civil War intruded on Sam's life very little. No one
under the age of twenty was being conscripted. After Lee sur-

rendered to Grant at Appomattox on April 9, 1865, the New York *Herald* beguiled its readers with the headline "OUT OF THE DRAFT, DAY OF REJOICING IN THE METROP-OLIS." "The great bug-bear of the wheel of conscription," it said, would now be wheeled "into that 'undiscovered country from whose bourn' it is to be hoped it will never return." The rejoicing, however, was short-lived. On April 15, a Saturday, Sam's attention was caught by a story in the *Herald* that began: "Assassination has been inaugurated in Washington." He read the rest of the story through tears. Lincoln had been his idol. He "felt that some great power for good had gone out of the world." A mood of depression enveloped him for days. When Lincoln's body was brought to New York on its way to inter-ment in Springfield, Sam waited in line for hours "for the privilege of looking upon his face." He would have been startled if he had been told that, before his own life was finished, some men would link his name to Lincoln's.

Sam was sixteen when he became involved in his first labor "struggle." He had joined Cigarmakers' Union Local 15 two years earlier, but the act had had no real significance for him. He was now working as a journeyman, as skilled craftsman were then known, in a cigar factory owned by a man named Stachel-berg. The men in the factory had some grievances they wanted to present to their employer. Sam was asked to speak for them. Possibly, it was because he spoke so well. But more likely, they chose him because he was young, and they thought that he had the least to risk. Mr. Stachelberg was outraged. He looked at the youngster speaking for men old enough to be his father, and said that he ought to be home where Mrs. Gompers could "dry you one behind the ears." He tried bullying Sam. When bullying failed, he invited him out for a beer. Sam refused to be diverted. The "case," as he referred to it, was won.

Sam was good at his craft. "This is Mr. Gompers," his em-ployer said to a visitor one day. "He is an agitator, but I don't give a damn. He makes me good cigars." The young cigarmaker "gloried in the swift sureness" with which he "could make cigars grow" in his fingers. He was able to practice his craft, he said, with such skill that it left him "free to think, talk, listen, or sing." In that respect at least, his craft was nearly idyllic.

Sam, in his hunger for learning, was haunting Cooper Union, but cigar factories were his real school. He thought of them as "labor forums." In New York, as in the Schwab factory in London, articles of unusual interest in newspapers and magazines, books, and pamphlets were read, analyzed, and argued over during the long day. The reader would be compensated in cigars by the other men for the time he had spent. An easy comradeship pervaded the factory. Opinions were exchanged freely; no dogmas ruled. When a man, enchanted by his particular truth, spoke too long or perhaps too arrogantly, the others silenced him by twisting the knives they used in cutting tobacco so as to produce a "whanging" sound. It was a democratic substitute for a chairman's gavel.

Sam would remember some of his shopmates of those early years for the rest of his life. There was Asmus Gerling, who had "the finest tenor voice" Sam would ever hear off the professional stage. When Gerling sang, no other sound was audible in the shop. Dan Harris, a former sailor who had served with Admiral Farragut, would generously bring in more lunch than he could use and share it with the "poorer boys." There was Al Unger the "man without an overcoat." Unger had calculated that five drinks of whiskey kept him "just as warm as an overcoat." He preferred the whiskey.

Many of those with whom Sam worked had been involved in European political struggles. Each new political convulsion in Europe started a fresh stream of such men, most of them revolutionists of one sort or another, into New York. Some had known Karl Marx in London, where the co-author of the *Communist Manifesto* presided over the International Workingmen's Association. They brought the aura of large affairs into Sam's life. The glow of their ideals, which contrasted so dramatically with the gray existence he knew, fired his imagination. Considering how his life was to be spent, his education probably could not have been better.

Meanwhile, he had started his own family. One day in 1866, a friend of his, Jack Polak, said to him: "Sam, I've got to go away for the summer. Will you look after my girl for me?" Sophia Julian worked at Stachelberg's, stripping tobacco leaves from plant stems, and Sam thought her olive-skinned face pretty. He looked after her cheerfully. She, too, was obviously pleased with the arrangement. One gathers that neither of them gave much thought to Jack Polak.

Sophia lived in Brooklyn. Sam's trips home after visiting Sophia were testimonials to his devotion. There was the ferry ride from Brooklyn to Manhattan, then a stagecoach to a point where he could get a streetcar. If it was late at night, and the stagecoach was no longer running, he would hitch a ride on the back of a milk wagon. But, on occasion, he had to walk through five miles of pitted, unlit streets in a neighborhood notorious for its "rough work." Of course, he had to be at his job shortly after daylight the next morning, but his sturdy physique, he said, gave him the "strength of an ox."

On January 27, 1867, Sam's seventeenth birthday, he and Sophia were with friends. It was suggested that they get married to celebrate the occasion. Early marriages were then common. Sophia, who was sixteen and a half, was willing, but it was too late in the day to reach a justice of the peace. The next day, however, "without consultation or announcement of plans," as Sam recalled the event, they went to Brooklyn's City Hall and joined their lives together. A son, Samuel J., was born to them on September 4, 1868. They were to have three more sons, two daughters, and their share of tragedy.

# 3

## *Choosing a Path*

The 1870's were to be decisive in Sam's life. He was twenty when they began. His first child, Sam J., was sixteen months old; a second child was on the way. Sam's responsibilities were accumulating. As he looked around him, he saw little to support the optimism with which the Gomperses had embarked for the United States. It did not appear that he would be able to do much better for his family than his father had done.

Many Americans were, of course, becoming immensely rich. In 1862, Congress had passed the Homestead Act; it granted 160 acres to anyone who settled in the frontier areas of the West. Some settlers would return with signs on their Conestoga wagons announcing sourly: "In God, we trusted. In Kansas, we busted." But the westward movement, encouraged by the railroads, which had been given tens of millions of acres by Congress, had developed into a wild speculative boom. Fabulous gold and silver lodes were being mined. Fortunes, it seemed, were being made overnight. Horatio Alger's *Luck and Pluck* romances extolled the virtues of success.

But there was another view. In 1873, Mark Twain and Charles Dudley Warner published *The Gilded Age*, which satirized the corruption that was the source of many new fortunes. One of their characters is Patrique O'Reillé, born Patrick O'Riley, who began his upward climb as the operator of a rum shop, gained influence in Tammany politics, and grew rich by selling shingle nails to New York City "at $3,000 a keg and eighteen gross of sixty-cent thermometers at $1,500 a dozen." This was minor skullduggery. The country was being looted on a grand scale. Collis Huntington, who owned the Central Pacific Railroad, thought it "only just and fair" to "pay money to have the right thing done." He arrived for one session of Congress with a trunk stuffed with $200,000 in cash. "I want to go to Egypt," said Madeleine Lee, the heroine of *Democracy*, a novel by Henry Adams. "Democracy has shaken my nerves to pieces."

Sam's world, too, was shaken, but flight to Egypt was no solution. A punishing workday of twelve hours or longer was common in factories, mills, and mines. Living costs had risen painfully. Between 1860 and 1870, average annual earnings had increased from $297 to $384, but higher living costs had reduced real earnings—what wages could buy—to $267. In the poor neighborhoods, where Sam and his friends lived, the misery was inescapable. Sam saw children, pitifully young, trudging to and from work. More than 1,500 children, some as young as four, were employed in the city's paper-collar factories alone. Some were so small that they had to stand on boxes to perform their jobs. The *New York Times* estimated, in October, 1869, that the city had 10,000 homeless children "who would suffer severely in winter and stormy weather." The tides of prosperity had left large islands of despair.

Efforts by workers to improve their conditions were resisted furiously. Late in 1869, workers on the Erie Railroad had gone on strike against wage cuts. The Erie was run by Jim Fisk, a notorious Wall Street buccaneer, and his equally notorious partner, Jay Gould. Fisk had threatened to organize 1,000 armed men to "put down" the strikers. The strikers, the *Times* reported, had "not manifested the slightest desire to disturb persons or property." Around the same time, a New England shoe manufacturer, unwilling to deal with his unionized workers, brought seventy-five Chinese laborers in from the Pacific Coast. The Chinese had "agreed" to work for $26 a month. "If for no other purpose than the breaking up of . . . unions," a writer for *Scribner's* magazine observed, "the advent of Chinese labor should be hailed with warm welcome by all those who have the true interests of . . . the laboring classes at heart." Sam could see little hope in the offing.

Then, in 1873, disaster struck. A financial crisis engulfed the country. It started on September 18, a dismally rainy day, when the banking firm of Jay Cooke, sometimes called the "Gibraltar" of American finance, closed its doors. Cooke's failure was nearly incredible to many Americans. It signaled the collapse of the speculative boom. Before the end of the year, 5,000 companies had failed. Sam daily met friends walking the streets desperately in search of work. "There is a good deal of suffering among working people already," the *Daily Graphic* reported on November 11, "and there will be a great deal more before midwinter." Workers joked bitterly about the *Graphic*'s advice to the poor to "keep clear of drinks which are the poor man's devil," and to "try to preserve as cheerful and hopeful a temper as possible." Public officials were just about as helpful. "They made gestures," Sam noted, "but did not give food to the hungry or solve the rent problem of those facing eviction."

On December 11, at Cooper Union, there was a meeting to protest the dreadful hardships workers were suffering. Sam, who was there, sensed a "stirring" toward solidarity. A "dramatic touch," he said, "fired our hearts and imaginations, and made us feel a part of the world-wide, age-long struggle against oppression." The "touch" was the authorization of a Committee of Safety, a name borrowed from the French Revolution, and intended, no doubt, at least partly, to shake the apathy of city officials. The city, in fact, began to show signs of uneasiness. Newspapers carried stories of threatened riots in other cities. A cartoon in one of them showed three jackasses, with a proclamation headed, "Down With Property," addressing a workers' meeting. There was a nervousness in the air. Peter McGuire, Sam's Cooper Union friend, now a Socialist, had been making incendiary speeches at street meetings. His father was persuaded to disown him publicly on the steps of a Catholic church. The *Times* denounced "labor demagogues." It was rumored that revolution was being plotted in the city.

The city was ripe for such rumors. In September, 1871, 25,000 people, Sam among them, had marched in a massive demonstration for the eight-hour day. Most of the marchers were workers, of course. "Eight Hours for Work, Eight Hours for Rest, Eight Hours for What We Will," their banners said. But the contingent that had attracted most notice consisted of sections of the International Workingmen's Association. It had carried a red flag and a banner inscribed with the slogan of the French Revolution: "Liberty, Equality, and Fraternity."

Later that year, Section 12 of the International had staged a memorial demonstration for several Frenchmen who had been executed by the Thiers Government. Members of Section 12 had worn red ribbons or ties. Victoria Woodhull and her sister Tennie C., attractive young women who scandalized New York in the early 1870's, had been conspicuously present. They published a newspaper, *Woodhull and Claflin's Weekly*, which advocated free love, anarchy, woman suffrage, and spiritualism, all calculated to outrage the proper. It had created a sensation by revealing a romance between the Reverend Henry Ward Beecher, the country's most prominent clergyman, and the wife of one of his parishioners.

Other radicals, some even more bizarre, were then agitating the city. One of them was Tom-ri-John, who published a paper, *Volcano*, in red ink on yellow paper, and whose three children were named Vesuvia, Eruptor, and Emancipator. The Woodhull sisters, and others like them, dominated Section 12 of the International. It was said that Karl Marx, in London, was appalled. Sam felt that they were "faddists," and "sensation-loving spirits." They were not working people," he was to write from a perspective gained by much struggle and pain. "They did not realize that labor issues were tied up with the lives of men, women, and children—issues not to be risked lightly."

For several years now, as "an onlooker," he had been attending meetings of the labor and radical groups with which the city teemed. Young Sam's mind was crowded with the visions of his revolutionary friends, but he sensed that something was escaping his grasp. The trade unions of the period, including his own, presented a confusing picture. Many of them were torn by conflicting ideologies. They lacked funds and stability; they called strikes on impulse; and they were essentially isolated from each other: corks bobbing haplessly on tides of discontent.

Many unions had been formed during the Civil War. In a single year, between December, 1863, and December, 1864, the number of unions in New York had shot up from sixteen to seventy-four. But many had fought losing battles against wage cuts in 1873; for all practical purposes, they had ceased to exist. In 1866, the National Labor Union (NLU) had been organized. It was the first real effort to establish a national labor federation in the United States. Its President, W. H. Sylvis, believed that workers could escape the hardships of the wage system by setting up producers' cooperatives. This was one of the many panaceas popular at the time. Sylvis's optimism verged on self-delusion. "Cooperation is taking hold on the minds of our members," he announced in 1867. "In many places, little else is talked about." He also put the National Labor Union deep into politics. By 1872, most of the cooperatives launched by NLU affiliates had failed or slipped into the hands of private owners; the NLU itself had become the property of political reformers.

In 1873, Sam's life took a turn he was to look back on with marveling gratitude. He went to work for David Hirsch and

Company, the only unionized cigar factory remaining in the city. There he met someone he later described as "the man whom I loved the most." His admiration for the "brain, heart, and character" of Karl Malcolm Ferdinand Laurrell, he wrote, was "boundless."

Laurrell was a Swede. He had become a cigarmaker in Copenhagen as a young man, after two years at sea, and had been deeply involved in European revolutionary movements; he had served as secretary of the Scandinavian section of the International Workingmen's Association. These were imposing credentials to Sam. Laurrell had become disenchanted with radicalism. Indeed, the views he expressed sometimes sounded amusingly jaundiced to his young friend. He lived in New Jersey, and he predicted that one day his son, Peter, would become governor of the state. "He has all the qualifications," he said. "He cusses, he cheats, and he lies." Laurrell, no doubt, was responsive to Sam's admiration, which must have been evident. He may also have seen in him a budding leader. At any rate, he undertook to save Sam from what he regarded as the pitfalls of radicalism. "Go to their (the Socialists') meetings by all means," he told him. "Listen to what they say and understand them, but do not join the Party."

Laurrell translated for him, paragraph by paragraph, his German copy of the *Communist Manifesto*, interpreting it for him as he went along; he wanted to give his admiring shopmate a "background philosophy," he said. Stimulated by Laurrell, Sam said, he studied German so that he would be able to read Marx, Engels, LaSalle, and other socialist writers for himself.

Regularly, at Hirsch, Sam would test some radical theory on Laurrell, and his tutor would carefully analyze and dismiss it, not always gently. He was a brusque man. Many trade unionists were then ready to subordinate their organizations to political ends. They were glad to admit to membership reformers and radicals who did not work at the trade in which the union

functioned. Laurrell thought that made no sense. He seems to
have understood, as later experiences would prove, that this
would only distract unions from the job of improving the conditions of their members in the "here and now." Sam must have
shown some resistance to this conclusion. "Study your union
card, Sam," Laurrell would say, "and if an idea doesn't square
with it, it ain't true." Laurrell pointed Sam in the direction
that would make him labor's pioneer in the "wilderness of
untried things." But it wasn't Laurrell's influence alone. "It is
not that which we read, hear, or see that makes us intelligent,"
Sam would say, but "that which we remember, analyze, and
utilize when the occasion arises." The occasion he would have
in mind occurred in the early days of 1874. It brought much
that he had been learning sharply into focus.

As an outgrowth of the meeting at Cooper Union on December 11, a demonstration had been planned by the Committee of
Safety for Tompkins Square on January 13. The police had
first granted a permit, then revoked it on the grounds that the
meeting "threatened public peace." The members of the Committee of Safety, however, mainly radicals, had dropped out of
sight. Almost immediately after workers marched into the
square, police, many of them mounted, charged down on them,
their night sticks swinging. Sam, who had arrived early, escaped
being clubbed by leaping into a cellarway. Laurrell was less
fortunate. He was months recovering from a policeman's blow.
A newspaper reported the story the next day under the headline
"DEFEAT OF THE COMMUNISTS." It thought that the
police had acted "wisely." But Sam was revolted by what he had
seen. Fifty years later, he would still think of it as the "Tompkins
Square outrage." He could not recall the scene without his
"blood surging in indignation at the brutality of the police that
day."

Something else stayed with Sam. For the radicals, he decided,
propaganda was "the chief end of life." "Practical results meant
nothing in their program," he said. "They were determined to

play a great part" and "unwilling to do the unostentatious, quiet, orderly things that make for progress." Their intoxication with doctrines, in his view, numbed them to realities.

His own life was seldom to be unostentatious and quiet, but he would never sacrifice for propaganda, or any other consideration, tangible gains for those he led. His emphasis on such gains, judged by its impact on American life, would prove to be the most genuinely revolutionary doctrine of all.

# 4

## Early Trials

Sam could see indignation turning the face of his brother
Henry red. Henry and his fellow cigarmakers had walked out
of their factory in protest against intolerable sanitation facilities.
A loathsome stench from the one water closet available to the
sixty men in the factory had become too much for them. Sam
knew how bad it was. Such conditions were all too common.
Yet, as president of Cigarmakers' Local 144, he felt that it was
his duty to tell the men to return to their jobs.

The union had rules, he said. The men would have to meet
and formally request approval of the union's Board of Administration to strike. It seemed unreasonable to Henry and the
others—all this nonsense about procedure. After all, they weren't
children. Nevertheless, they yielded. They returned to work the
next morning, though only briefly, and held their meeting. That
night the union's Board of Administration approved their request. Their strike, as it turned out, won improvements within
a day. Few of the union's strikes were so brief or ended so
happily. But it was the beginning of effective unionism for the

cigarmakers. Previously, many strikes had begun when one worker, more sensitive to abuses, or more rebellious, than his fellows, stood up from his bench and announced: "I'm going to quit. Any man that don't is a scab." It was emotionally satisfying, Sam knew, but the strikes generally failed, the men suffered, and the cause of unionism was damaged.

Late in 1875, Local 144 had been formed by merging the skeletal remains of Local 15 and another cigarmakers' organization. Sam, though only twenty-five, had been elected its president. Other men had begun to turn to him. Perhaps it was the strength radiated by his short, powerful body or the passion of his convictions. No doubt, his deep, resonant voice helped. In the period before the "microphone," a big voice was a commanding asset.

Adolph Strasser, who worked with Sam at Hirsch, had been elected the union's financial secretary. It was rumored that he had come from an affluent Hungarian or Austrian family. His bearing was aristocratic. "He did not make cigars as one who had learned the trade in his youth," Sam observed. Strasser, like Laurrell, had been prominent in the International Workingmen's Association. Now he thought that socialism was "sophistry." Like Laurrell, he tended to be brusque. He would, in time, be referred to as the "Bismarck" of the cigarmakeres. But he shared Laurrell's high regard for Sam. He also shared the conviction that, if workers were to have a better future, it would be won by trade unions. He had lost faith in theories for transforming society. "We are opposed to theorists," Strasser would tell a Senate Committee on Education and Labor in 1883. "We have no ultimate ends. We are all practical men." They were members of a small but growing band. They were making the cigarmakers a model for other unions.

Sam's office in the union carried no salary. But night after night, after his long day at the cigarmakers' bench, he would be out spreading the gospel of unionism at meetings, in saloons, wherever men could be reached. When strikes demanded his attention, he would stop at picket lines on his way to and from his job at Hirsch. One morning, at a picket line, he was arrested. He had violated no law; he had simply been talking to the pickets. The judge refused him time to get counsel. The sentence was a $10 fine or ten days in jail. Sam would not have paid the fine if his "life depended on it," he said. He was sent to the Tombs, a prison as forbidding as its name, but his friends at Hirsch, who were told about his arrest, came around and paid his fine.

The union's unpaid president had other chores. Sundays often found him struggling with an old Multigraph machine to turn out copies of the union's constitution for its members. Some critics said that he and his friends were "democracy mad."

Sam had been searching for the "language, the methods, and the fundamentals" that would permit the building of effective and durable trade unions. He felt now that he had found them. They would be "pure and simple" trade unions made up of workers in their trades; they would exclude political propagandists and reformers who were not employed in these trades and who joined labor organizations primarily to use them for political ends; they would strive for discipline and financial stability; and they would concentrate on improving the living standards of their members. This concept, now commonplace, was considered treasonous by the radicals; they saw the labor movement as the seedbed in which their ideas could most easily flourish.

But, for the union, adversity always seemed to wait in ambush. Local 144's membership was 1,200 in 1875. The next year, unemployment cut it to 500. Two-thirds of the city's cigar factories were closed. Many cigarmakers had been without jobs for months. The effects of the depression started by the panic three years earlier were still being felt. Workers all over the country had suffered repeated wage cuts. They were becoming increasingly restive. Other matters pulled at the country's attention. In 1876, there was a storm over the Presidential election. Samuel Jones Tilden, on all the evidence, had won, but Republican election officials in Louisiana and Florida, states still occupied by federal troops, voided enough Tilden ballots to switch the state's electoral votes to Rutherford Birchard Hayes. It gave him a one-vote majority in the Electoral College. In the same year, at a fair in Philadelphia, Brazil's Emperor Dom Pedro picked up Alexander Graham Bell's new invention, held it to his ear, and exclaimed: "My God, it talks!" In Montana's Black Hills, Sioux Chief Rain-in-the-Face, whose warriors had massacred General Custer's troopers, cut out and ate Custer's heart. Workers' problems did not seem especially urgent. "Is not a dollar a day sufficient to buy bread?" asked Henry Ward Beecher, the clergyman, who was paid $20,000 a year by the Plymouth Church. "Water costs nothing and a man who cannot live on bread is not fit to live. A family may live, laugh, love, and be happy that eats bread in the morning with good water, and water with good bread at noon and water and bread at night."

A while earlier, Thomas Nast, the famous cartoonist of *Harper's Weekly*, had drawn a political zoo. It showed labor as the goat. In 1877, the goat butted. "WAR ON THE RAILROADS," newspaper headlines announced alarmingly, "MORE RIOT AND BLOODSHED," "THE MOB AT BUFFALO," "BLOODSHED IN SAN FRANCISCO." It started on July 16 when the Baltimore and Ohio Railroad reduced wages for the third time in three years. That evening, at Martinsburg, West Virginia, the B & O workers struck. The strike spread swiftly, and a few days later, when the Pennsylvania Railroad also reduced wages, it seemed to engulf railroads all across the country. It was a spontaneous action. The railroad unions were weak. The workers had simply been pushed too hard. In Pittsburgh, fifty-seven strikers and soldiers were killed in a wild battle. One hundred and twenty-six locomotives were destroyed. In Baltimore, twelve workers were killed by the Sixth

Maryland Militia. In Cleveland, John Hay, who was to become the country's Secretary of State, wrote to his father-in-law, "The very devil seems to have entered into the lower classes of workingmen, and there are plenty of scoundrels to encourage them to all lengths." President Hayes ordered out federal troops in six states. The country seemed to be throbbing with an impulse toward rebellion.

"The sky of Pittsburgh," Sam wrote, "reddened by fires, brought us the message that human aspiration had not been killed or cowed." But he recognized that it had no relation to the "constructive methods" in which he had placed his faith. On July 26, he spoke at a mass meeting at Cooper Union. It had been called to express sympathy with the railroad strikers. The day was miserably hot, but, according to the *Times* report, the meeting was jammed. It passed a resolution urging the formation of a national federation of trade unions, "so that combined capital can be successfully resisted and overcome." Sam was the last speaker. "Mr. Gompers, of the Cigarmakers," said the *Times*, "made a miserable fist of it."

Some months later, *Puck*, a magazine published in New York, carried a cartoon showing Sam running toward Concordia Hall. "I cannot stop," it had him saying, "I am busy, for I am on strike." He was, in fact, desperately busy. He had been to a convention, in Rochester, of the Cigarmakers' International Union. He had seen an opportunity to have Strasser elected the international union's president, and had wired him: "Will you accept presidency? Election sure. Salary $250." It was the salary for a year. Strasser had agreed. Sam returned to New York in high spirits, but immediately found himself confronted by a chilling problem. Cigarmakers in the city's tenement shops, driven by economic misery, had gone on strike. Sam knew their misery. In the tenements, whole families worked together, and he had seen "the little children with their young-old faces and their work-weary figures." He had come to regard child labor as criminal. But the tenement workers had never cooperated with the union. There had been no preparation for the strike. Like the railroad workers, and probably inspired by them, they had simply rebelled. Local 144, which had $4,000 in its treasury, carefully hoarded for its own strikes, was less than overjoyed. It decided, nevertheless, to support the tenement-house workers. Sam, as president of the union, became the strike leader. It was to be a strike he would never forget.

His responsibilities were all but overwhelming. "The Gompers are built of oak," his wife would tell friends; he would need that oaklike quality in the months ahead. The employers, in retaliation, had locked out most of Local 144's members. More than eleven thousand men were out on strike. Some forty thousand women and children were dependent on them. Relief stores were opened by the union. Meat and bread were distributed daily; each family was given a basket of groceries once a week. The tenement-house employers evicted strikers' families, some in the middle of winter, and rooms had to be found for them. The strike was the first thoroughly organized one in American history.

Sam, as the *Puck* cartoon suggested, moved through it at a dead run. Meetings, picket lines, and the innumerable details of administering relief to the strikers demanded his attention. In addition, the union had taken over a cigar factory to employ its men. Members had approved the project on the condition that Sam would act as foreman. He had been earning $18 a week at Hirsch. He accepted the foreman's job for $12, then the average earnings of a cigarmaker, and he paid 10 per cent of that as a strike assessment. The cooperative factory was more than two miles from his home. He walked to it, sometimes in sleet and snow, then to his meetings at night, and finally home, because he couldn't afford the fare. "Those of us who helped to build pioneer organizations," he would tell people years later, "fought a fight of intensity and desperation little dreamed of in this modern period."

But the most valiant efforts were not sufficient. The strike
crumbled. Employers refused to hire its leaders. For Sam, like
the Spitalfields workers of his childhood, there was "no work
to do." Twenty-eight years old, the president of his union for
more than two years, a person of some prominence in the city,
he walked the streets looking for work.

Jack Polak, who had introduced Sam to Sophia eleven years
earlier, now re-entered their lives in a strange way. Sam had
been unemployed for nearly four months. He had pawned, or
sold, everything of value in his possession to feed his family,
which now included five children. A sixth child was expected.
Sophia kept them alive with soup that she made of flour and
water and seasoned with salt and pepper. All of them were often
hungry. Their youngest child, a girl, was ill. One night, when
Sam returned home, his wife told him that Polak had been
there. He had offered, in the name of some mysterious party,
$30 a week for three months if Sam would quit the union.
"Well, what did you tell him?" he asked. Sophia was upset.
Plainly, she had reason to be. "Of course, I took the money,"
she said. "What do you suppose I did, with one child dying and
another coming?" Speechless, Sam collapsed into a chair. "Good
God, Sam!" she said. "How could you ask such a question?
Don't you know that I resented the insult?"

But Sam was becoming increasingly desperate. Once, he said,
he was ready "to commit murder." On February 28, 1878, he
returned home, after a day of fruitless job hunting, to find that
his sixth child had been born, and that there had been nobody
to help Sophia or the infant. He rushed out to find the doctor
paid by the Hand-in-Hand Society, a Hebrew mutual aid organization to which he belonged, but the man was not at home.
He sought help from another physician who lived nearby. This
physician refused to be bothered. "I do not feel like it," he
said, "and I won't do it." "Yes, you will," Sam said, reaching
out for the man's coat collar. "You will come now with me or

you will never make another move." The physician looked at Sam, a menacing figure in his desperation, and decided quickly, as many others would, that he meant exactly what he said.

Sam found jobs but they didn't last. The manufacturers' association brought pressure on one employer to fire him. Another employer offered to pay him $25 a week as a foreman and half of what could be saved if Sam would persuade the cigarmakers in the shop to accept a wage reduction. "Good night," Sam said abruptly, and, since he didn't have a nickel for carfare in his pocket, walked home. Years earlier, as a member of a little group of high-minded trade unionists known as the Economic and Sociological Club, he had subscribed to the following pledge: "Under no circumstances will we accept public office or become interested in any business venture of any character or accept any preferment outside of the labor movement." It was a pledge Sam had not the slightest desire to violate.

As his reputation and influence grew, he would receive many imposing offers. John R. Dos Passos, a famous New York lawyer and financier, would offer him a guarantee of a million dollars in ten years if he would accept the presidency of an industrial accident insurance company. Promoters with an immense land concession in Mexico would ask him to head a development company at $50,000 a year. There were numerous offers of high political posts. Sam would decline them all, a little baffled on occasion that people should think him interested in a career other than the one he had chosen. His loyalty to the cause of labor was religious in its intensity. During one ten-month period, when his father was the foreman of a shop in which he worked, he refused to visit his father's home.

In 1878, it was Laurrell who came to his rescue. "I will bulldoze that boss of mine," he said, "and make him give you a job." Sam protested that this might make trouble for him; Laurrell answered: "You are already bad friends with the bosses. Can you afford to make bad friends with me?" Laurrell came to his rescue in another way. Sam, "burning with sentiment" induced by his bitter experiences, was tempted to turn to a more radical course. What saved him, he said, was Laurrell's caution: "Never permit sentiment to lead you. Let intellect dominate action."

# 5

## *You Can't Build on Bubbles*

In Sam Gompers's shop, as they rolled cigars, they were taking turns reading an exciting new book by an itinerant journalist and typesetter named Henry George. It was called *Progress and Poverty*. It dealt with economics, but it was a best-seller in 1879, and it was probably read by more workers than any other book on the "dismal science" in history. George's single-tax theory held that all economic woes could be eliminated by taxing the social value of land; that is, the value added by the growth of society. It seemed marvelously simple. Moreover, his indictment of society could easily be confirmed by what was visible all around them. There has been "a prodigious increase in wealth-producing power," George wrote, but this increase, which "is still going on at an accelerating ratio, has no tendency to extirpate poverty or to lighten the burden of those compelled to toil."

The country, again in the midst of boom times, was emerging as a great industrial power. Smoke stacks were becoming commonplace on the skylines of eastern towns and cities. Factory workers now outnumbered those in agriculture.

A new aristocracy, based on booming industry and commerce, had come into being. Andrew Carnegie had established himself as the country's leading steelmaker. John D. Rockefeller, whose Standard Oil Trust had gobbled up most of its rivals during, and after, the panic of 1873, was well on the way to what would eventually be a billion-dollar fortune. The House of Morgan dominated American finance. Suddenly, it seemed, a legion of multimillionaires had materialized. Most of them were of humble origin; it was as if all the waifs in Horatio Alger's *Luck and Pluck* stories had justified their creator's gaudiest expectations. It had become fashionable in New York's "marble palaces" to serve six or seven choice wines at dinner, a different one with each course. There were elaborate fancy-dress balls. The choice and preparation of costumes for one of these, according to the *Times*, "disturbed the sleep and occupied the waking hours of social butterflies, both male and female, for over six weeks." It was said of another that it was superior to those of the "ancient nobility of the old world."

Meanwhile, more than 25 per cent of the country's workers were still laboring eleven hours or more a day, and improvement in earnings, despite the boom, had been negligible. Winslow Homer had drawn a picture, *Bell Time*, showing workers, some bent with age and some not yet in their teens, leaving a New England mill after a thirteen-hour day. This was all too common. The hovels abutting mills and factories bulged with a vast horde of new immigrants. Many had been brought to the United States under labor contracts to ensure an ample supply of "cheap" hands. Their presence added to the difficulty of organizing unions. A newspaper cartoon of the time, captioned "Supply and Demand," showed immigrant workers tilting the scales against strikers.

Thousands of men were constantly drifting across the country in search of work. The "tramp" had become a familiar figure in American life. Walt Whitman, who had heard "America singing," now found himself troubled by unpleasant discords. "If the United States, like the countries of the old world, are also to grow vast crops of poor, desperate, dissatisfied, nomadic, miserably-waged populations," he wrote in Camden, New Jersey, to which he had retired, partially paralyzed, "then our republican experiment, notwithstanding all its surface successes, is at heart an unhealthy failure."

Sam's sense of injustice required no literary honing. Poverty had been his companion since boyhood; hunger was no stranger to him. Even now, as a skilled cigarmaker, he was hardly in enviable circumstances. He and his family were still living in a crowded East Side flat. His oldest son, Samuel J., was eleven, and Sam and Sophia had talked over how long they would be able to keep young Sam in school. "We wanted our children to have opportunities denied to us," he said. But necessity would prove to be a rude prod. The boy would leave school three years later to work in a print shop, and, after that, his father would seldom see him except on Sundays. As for Sam, he was still walking in broken shoes, but they were taking him to the center of the national stage.

In 1881, the Cigarmakers' International Union chose Sam to represent it at a conference of trade unions that was to be held in Pittsburgh in November for the purpose of establishing a national labor federation. Sam looked forward to it as a possible opportunity "to do something for all the wage-earners." The pattern of his life was now irreversibly set. He "wanted most intensely to be of service," he said.

In a photograph of Sam taken in this period, his black hair, combed straight back, comes down on his neck well below his ears. A handlebar mustache gives him a rakish look. He is wearing a Prince Albert coat, then considered an emblem of dignity among working men, but his trousers are baggy and a little too long, possibly because his thick torso and short legs were difficult to fit. There is a suggestion in his appearance of what one journalist referred to as "anthropoid strength," and there is no doubt that he was not the kind of person with whom one lightly invited a brawl. One night at Justus Schwab's saloon, a gathering place for radicals in New York, Johann Most, a fiery anarchist, goaded Sam by insulting his associates, and Sam took him by the throat and shook him thoroughly. "Gompers got more than Most," a newspaper wit commented.

Most was a romantic figure. Four years older than Sam, he had been in and out of European jails for revolutionary activity. His face was deformed, but that detracted from neither his appeal nor his ardor. He mounted the platform at one workers' meeting, carrying a rifle, and announced: "A few hundred armed workers can make the social revolution." "One could almost smell the gunpowder," a journalist wrote.

"It was the genius of Samuel Gompers," a student of the period observed, "that, surrounded by revolutionary refugees and zealous utopian intellectuals, he grasped the central reality of American life." The chasm between the dreams men had brought to this country and their harsh, chattel-like existence had raised wild political fevers. Sam, now thirty-one, was familiar with all of them: the Marxian socialists, the anarchists preaching "propaganda of the deed," those who thought that producers' cooperatives offered the only escape from the inequities of the wage system, the Greenbackers who believed passionately that the solution to society's ills was to be found in "cheap" money, and the proponents of a variety of other panaceas. Sam had listened attentively to radicals of every kind, and he had read their works, for more than a dozen years. He found all of them hopelessly impractical. It was ridiculous to believe, he had concluded, that "we shall go to bed one night under the present system, and the morrow morning wake up with a revolution in full blast, and the next day organize a heaven on earth. That is not the way progress is made," he said. "That is not the way the interests of the human family are advanced." He felt that working people were too urgently in need of immediate improvements in their conditions to forgo them for some nebulous utopia. By 1881, his own philosophy had been completely thought out. It revealed the influence of Laurrell and Strasser and his own experiences with the cigar-makers. He was convinced that progress could be made only by concentrating on practical and limited gains. He believed, moreover, that reducing the workday by an hour and adding twenty-five cents to a day's pay were more valuable than the finest revolutionary rhetoric. His emphasis on "more, more now" and his disdain for revolutionary theorists were to keep him embroiled in disputes with extremists of the right and left throughout his life.

The Pittsburgh conference was Sam's first experience with a national gathering of unionists from various trades. He was already well known in New York. In Pittsburgh, he emerged as a national figure. On the first day of the conference, while the credentials committee was preparing its report, he was asked to speak. His remarks reflected his commitment to the practical. He was there, he told the delegates, "not to air his opinions but to work, not to build a bubble but to lay the foundations for a superstructure that would be solid, and that would be a true federation of trade unions." Apparently, he made a strong impression. That night, he went to a meeting to hear a Greenbacker known as "Beeswax." The Greenbackers were then popular. In 1878, in alliance with the Grange, a farm organization, and some trade unions, they had polled around a million votes and had elected fifteen congressmen. Sam saw them as another distraction. At the end of the meeting, several of his fellow delegates, who were present, offered their congratulations to him. "What for?" he asked. They informed him that he was to be nominated for the presidency of the new labor federation. If he had any visions of glory, they were premature. Ironically, the next morning, the *Pittsburgh Commercial Gazette* attacked him as a "rule or ruin" socialist. It was said that the story had been inspired by a supporter of another candidate. Sam, who had never been affiliated with any socialist organization, even in his youth, was indignant. He denounced the attack on him as a fiction, but he thought it unwise, under the circumstances, to accept the nomination. He did not want the office with his motives under a cloud, he said.

The new organization formed in Pittsburgh called itself the Federation of Organized Trades and Labor Councils of the United States and Canada. It turned out to be the forerunner of the American Federation of Labor, and its major significance, in restrospect, seems to have been that it introduced Sam to the national scene. It had no full-time officer, no headquarters, and hardly any money. The secretary was authorized to purchase 1,000 letterheads; these constituted one of the few tangible evidences of its existence. The main emphasis of its program was on legislation. It called for a compulsory-education law, for a law prohibiting the labor of children under the age of fourteen, and for various other reforms for which organized labor pioneered in the United States. It decided that, at future conferences or congresses, "no paper shall be read except those which are required for legislative purposes." Sam's comment is interesting: "In those early days," he wrote, "not more than a half-dozen people had grasped the concept that economic organization and control over economic power were the fulcrum which made possible influence and power in all other fields." Popularizing that concept was to be part of his distinctive contribution.

Sam did not leave Pittsburgh as the federation's president, but he was elected first vice-president of its legislative committee, which was given the responsibility for managing the affairs of the federation. It was a signal honor for one so young.

In 1882, he was elected president of the legislative committee, and, because the committee was responsible for managing the federation, he became, in effect, the federation's leader. In 1883, when it convened in New York, he was the chairman. The bloody 1877 strikes were still fresh in his mind when he made his opening speech. It was bitter. Employers would, if they could, "subjugate the workingmen and prevent them from organizing for mutual protection," he said. "The strong arm of government is on their side and against us. The police and the military are used against labor, and even the good will of the order-loving citizens is employed to crush us." Then, as now, many people thought it more important to preserve order than to correct injustice.

But it was already evident that the federation could not be expected to alter this state of affairs. It remained little more than a letterhead.

In 1885, when it met in Washington, D.C., only a handful of delegates were present. For Sam, momentarily in gloom at the flickering out of an organization for which he had had high hopes, there was one compensation. It was the oyster season, and an excellent seafood restaurant was nearby. "I ate oysters every day," he reported. But, before another year had passed, this formidable little man, so zealous for his cause, would be concerned with larger matters.

# 6

## The Courage to Wait

The room, located in a shed on East Eighth Street in Manhattan, measured 8 by 10 feet. Sam had used it as the editor of the *Picket*, a rather primitive four-page paper published by the Cigarmakers' Union. The type for its title had been designed so that every vertical line was topped belligerently with a spearhead, and Sam had been told by a leading journalist of the day that he seemed to do his editing "with an axe." In any event, he was now using the shed for a more ambitious project. In December, 1886, what remained of the Federation of Organized Trades and Labor Unions and a number of other unions had met in Columbus, Ohio, and established the American Federation of Labor. Sam had been the unanimous choice of the delegates for the Federation's presidency. This was not entirely a tribute to his abilities. "My job as president," he noted, "was coveted by no one. There was much work, little pay, and very little honor."

At the outset, the new organization, like its predecessor, was little more than a name. It bore little resemblance to the power-

50

ful and prestigious labor organizations of today. It had only $160.52 in its treasury. The unions affiliated with it were unstable and poor. Many of them couldn't afford even to pay their officers. These men worked at their trades, as Sam had during the five years that he had been president of Local 144, and they devoted long hours Sundays and at night to the cause. At Columbus, many of them had worn Prince Albert coats and silk hats as badges of self-respect, but a knowing pickpocket would not have bothered with them. Sam was the new Federation's only full-time officer. He had to function as its organizer, strategist, and spokesman, also as its clerk and errand boy.

Only one man approached Sam in importance in the Federation. Peter J. McGuire had shed his socialist beliefs. In 1881, he had organized the Brotherhood of Carpenters and Joiners. At Columbus, he had been elected secretary of the Federation. The eloquence and passion he had displayed as a young man at Cooper Union were now being used in the service of the new trade union movement. He was, said Sam, "the only other officer of the Federation who felt a real responsibility for the work" that had to be done.

Sam had been voted a salary of $1,000 a year, about as much as he was then earning as a cigarmaker. It was his first salaried trade union office; he had accepted it with some misgivings. He knew the "poverty of the wage-earner," he said, and he "did not like to think of accepting money" for his services. It was a while before he received any. The payment of his salary did not start until March. "My family and I just put ourselves in the psychological position of a strike or lockout," he said in recalling the hardships his career had imposed. "Many a time, the children had to stay home while shoes or clothes were being repaired. Many a night, the children went to bed hungry." A gold, diamond-studded medal he had received from the Ancient Order of Foresters in 1873 was frequently in the pawn shop. He could get as much as $50 for it, but he rarely "asked

for more than five or ten," he said; he would have had difficulty in redeeming it. "Mother" Gompers accepted whatever
sacrifices were required with a pioneer woman's fortitude, and
her pride equaled his. When there was no food in the house,
she concealed the fact from visitors by keeping covered pots,
containing only water, simmering on the stove.

The Gomperses were a close-knit and loving family. Sundays
would sometimes find Sam playing with his four sons—Sam,
Henry, Abe, and Al—at a picnic ground near their home. "The
brief hours I had at home were very happy," Sam wrote of the
early years of his domestic life. "Mother usually had a baby in
her arms. Many an hour, she sang lullabies and crooned cradle
songs in her soft musical voice. It soothed baby and all of us."
Somehow, at the beginning of his presidency of the Federation,
when there was no income, they "managed."

The threadbare office accurately mirrored the Federation's
condition. A battered kitchen table, which Sam had brought
down from his home, now on Sixty-Ninth Street, served as a
desk. His chair was a box. Tomato crates, donated by a friendly
grocer, substituted for filing cabinets. The office had other
shortcomings. The principal one during the first winter was
that it had no stove, and a numbing chill seeped up through the
shed's brick floor. To make matters worse, Sam often had to
walk to his office through the bleak winter mornings, a distance
of over three miles. Carfare was still an indulgence he couldn't
always afford.

Newspapers sometimes referred to Sam as a "demagogue"
and a "dangerous man." In a sense, these descriptions were
justified. He was set on arousing workers against an industrial
tyranny that used people "without regard to their needs or aspirations as individuals." He found this loathsome. He loved
men, he said, and "a sort of passion" surged through him when
he saw them treated "unjustly." He regarded trade unions as
the "natural, orderly, and democratic" means by which workers
could escape the degradation in which the new industrialism

had imprisoned them. Unions were for him the "legitimate heirs" to all the "struggles of the human family for freedom and progress."

In the 1880's, such views, no matter how sedately expressed, were shocking to most people. It was a period when any effort by labor to claim rights for itself was considered impudent, if not seditious, and union leaders were extravagantly abused. In New York, a bill to limit the workday of streetcar employees to twelve hours was denounced by Theodore Roosevelt, then a state senator, as "purely socialistic." John Hay published a rather awkward novel in which a union organizer, whom he named Ananias Offit, was portrayed as a "greasy apostle of labor." It was a common caricature. In newspaper cartoons, union organizers were regularly shown either as bearded anarchists, armed with knives or bombs, or as bloated parasites. The obvious contradiction seemed not to bother the editors. But such abuse was a relatively minor matter. Everywhere in the country, private armies of spies and thugs, most notably the Pinkertons, were used to break strikes. The courts, police, state militias, and even federal troops were frequently employed against unions.

The atmosphere was especially hostile when Sam took up his new duties as president of the American Federation of Labor. Two events in 1886 had inflamed what would now be called the Establishment. Henry George had run for mayor of New York as a labor candidate. Sam was fond of Henry George. Indeed, they were to become warm friends. Deep in discussion of the single tax, socialism, and trade unionism, they would go cycling together on Sundays. George, like Sam, was short and rather bristly; they must have made an odd sight as they pedaled through the city streets. Sam had questioned the wisdom of those who were "anxious for workingmen to rush into politics." Previous experiences of this kind had been disastrous, he argued. "Never mind reviews, Brother Gompers," a labor journalist had replied. "Let the dead past bury the dead.

The world is whirling. Now is on the march. . . . Today is not yesterday and tomorrow will be different from both." "There was," said Sam, "a curious determination to disregard experience." Nevertheless, he had worked for George with furious energy. He had served as secretary of the Henry George Legions and as director of a Speakers' Bureau, and he had organized a great pre–Election Day rally. The campaign had been regarded, with some justification, as a confrontation of classes. "Do not attempt to spread the schism wider," Sam had warned the Democratic candidate, "lest, instead of using this constitutional and legal method, men may turn to less constitutional." The Democrat, aided by vote-stealing on a large scale by the corrupt Tammany machine, had won, but George had polled sixty-eight thousand votes, some eight thousand more than Theodore Roosevelt, the Republican candidate. Nerves, in the centers of power, had been shaken.

However, far more hostility to labor had been generated by the Haymarket Square bombing, in Chicago, the previous May. It had sent waves of antilabor hysteria billowing across the country. On May 1, in Chicago, ninety thousand workers had struck for the eight-hour day. It was part of a nation-wide effort. Two days later, at the McCormick reaper works, police killed one striker and seriously wounded others. The next night, on May 4, there was a protest meeting at Haymarket Square. The speakers were mainly anarchists, who were influential in the city, but, while their speeches were inflammatory, the meeting was peaceful. Chicago's mayor, Carter Harrison, was present for a while, and saw nothing to disturb him. The crowd began to disperse, urged on by the threat of rain, when squads of policemen advanced on the open wagon serving as a platform. Samuel Fielden, an English-born anarchist, who was speaking, protested, "We are peaceable." At that moment, someone threw a bomb. It exploded among the police, killing one of them and wounding many more. Eight anarchists were indicted for murder, and seven of them were sentenced to death, although the only evidence against them was the nature of the statements they had made. The judge, Joseph E. Gary, in his charge to the jury, explicitly conceded this. "The conviction proceeds upon the ground," he said, that the defendants had, "by speech and print, advised large classes . . . to commit murder," and had left "the commission, the time, and place, and when, to the individual will."

Shortly after Sam became president of the AFL, he went to Chicago to ask Governor Ogelsby for clemency for the condemned men. Some Chicago unionists, fearful of the consequences, disapproved of his action. "I abhor anarchy," Sam wrote to a friend who reported this, "but I also abhor injustice when meted out even to the most despicable being on earth." He was determined, he added, to "maintain the dignity and honor of our organization, and withal, to be manly and not cringing."

Few of Sam's radical critics appreciated his devotion to justice or his courage in defending it.

But his courage, physical as well as moral, was a major ingredient in the magnetism that drew men to him. During his first year as head of the Federation, he was presiding at a union gathering in Albany, New York, when a hothead, representing a rival union group, leaped to the platform, a pistol in his hand, and advanced to shoot him. "Give me that pistol," Sam commanded, his eyes fixed on the would-be assassin, and the man, suddenly meek, surrendered it to him. "The gun was quite the largest thing I ever saw," Sam later told a friend jokingly. "It looked to be longer than a telegraph pole, and the bore seemed big enough for a horse to walk through." He enjoyed dramatizing things. He had been nervous, he confessed, but felt that he "could not afford to show it." Nervousness was a quality seldom, if ever, associated with him.

Some years later, when coal miners in West Virginia went on strike against conditions they found intolerable, a judge issued an injunction that, in effect, denied the miners the rights of free speech and assembly. Sam, who regarded this as

This photo of Gompers was taken by a detective in West Virginia in 1897, when the labor leader defied an injunction that denied miners their right of free speech. (AFL-CIO *News*)

judicial tyranny, went into West Virginia mining communities where he calmly defied the injunction. He spoke from wagon tops on mountain roads and wherever else he could be of service. "I hold a jail more roomy in the expression of my convictions than the whole world if I were to submit to repression," he said.

He had little patience for those who chose to submit. An organizer from Wisconsin who had been assigned to West Virginia before Sam's arrival there, and who was worried about a jail sentence, went over to Kentucky, where he wired: "No doubt, you know of the injunction issued by Judge Jackson forbidding organizers holding public meetings in West Virginia. I am here in Kentucky and want your further advice what I shall do." "We want organizers in West Virginia," Sam replied. "If you prefer remaining in Kentucky, I prefer that you return to Wisconsin."

Sam had written to one of his close associates, Andrew Furuseth, the gaunt, Lincolnesque leader of the seamen's union, about plans to lead a demonstration of miners in West Virginia. Furuseth had replied:

By all means, march. There is a way to make such a formation of the marching column that the deputies cannot very well stop it. You remember the wedge of the Norsemen and the Macedonians formed about thus: Arms interlocking in such a way as to form one solid mass—no hands or arms outside, the parties held in position by the unarmed ones, moving ahead slowly. . . .

The man at the head of the wedge might get pushed pretty badly, so might most of the outside ones; yet no force of deputies could stop such a wedge except by wholesale killing, and they could not do that. It would be unprovoked slaughter. . . . Of course, I know who will have to take the head of the wedge, but I know him and I know that he has the courage to do it if he thinks that it is needed.

Courage of another kind was required during the early days

of the Federation. The organization was given little chance to succeed even by those who sympathized with its purposes. Some of the Federation's affiliated unions doubted that it was worth supporting. The International Typographical Union voted not to pay the per capita tax of one-half cent per member a month. Sam's own Cigarmaker's International Union fell behind in its payments. "Do you think it the wisest policy," Sam asked his old friend Adolph Strasser, "to assist in starving the Federation out of existence?" He found it discouraging. "Money is coming in very slowly," he wrote to the Federation's treasurer in April, 1887. "I will have shortly to decide upon giving up the position and take a post at my trade or starve." He had served the labor movement without pay for years, he said, and he was willing to continue to do so, "but with a large family depending upon me for support, I cannot give my entire time without recompense." A year after the Federation was formed, it had only $25.95 in its treasury; its expenses, which Sam carefully itemized, had included $8.50 for a stove and pipe, $2 for a secondhand desk, and $1 for pine wood used in constructing files.

Sam had pleaded with the Federation's Executive Council for permission to hire an office boy. He was spending time "running errands," he said, that "could be put to much better advantage." The Executive Council consented, and Henry, Sam's second-oldest son, came to work for the Federation at $3 a week. Like his father, however, the boy wasn't always paid. They walked to work together, carrying their lunch with them, and often they walked back. Henry borrowed ink from a nearby school when they were short of it. When Sam's one pair of shoes needed repairing, Henry took them to the shoe shop while the president of the AFL wore an old pair of house slippers. The practice was common in the Gompers family. "There were no changes," Sam noted.

In the cramped shed on East Eighth Street, he carried on a prodigious correspondence. All letters had to be written by hand, and he wrote almost incessantly. Little authority had been vested in the presidency of the Federation. Primarily, he functioned as a propagandist and counsel. He urged unions to inscribe "affiliated with the American Federation of Labor" on their letterheads. He advised groups on how to proceed with organizing unions. He cautioned against hastily called strikes. "Have the courage to wait," he wrote to one union. "Bide your time until you can take practical action." "Do not strike in haste and repent at your leisure," he advised another union. "Strengthen your position so that you may have a good chance of victory before you strike. This may be a slow process but it is the surest, in the end, and the quickest and by far the safest. It may be galling to wait for victory but defeat is worse."

His caution was criticized. Several of his close associates were unhappy about the slowness of progress; a California union leader dismissed the Federation as "impotent." The charge would recur periodically during the Federation's early years, but Sam was convinced that "the foundation of a great movement" was being laid. He, too, was eager for progress, but he had the "courage to wait." He did not want to undertake campaigns that were beyond the resources of the organization, and he did not believe in empty gestures. He was concerned with practical results.

# 7

## A Seeker of Men

On an uncomfortably hot summer day, in the hills of Pennsylvania, Sam Gompers was having difficulty as he trudged along a railroad track on his stumpy legs. He was sweaty and dirty. He had left Pittsburgh that morning on a train for Connellsville, where he was scheduled to address a meeting of coke workers. He habitually read on trains; he had become immersed in a book. Unfortunately, the train had gone seven miles beyond his station before the conductor had come by to check his ticket. Now, slipping and stumbling occasionally on the uneven footing, his shirt clinging moistly to his chest, he was making his way back along the railroad. He reached Connellsville wilted and weary, but he went immediately to the meeting, which was already in progress. There, for two hours, his musical baritone voice sounded the gospel of trade unionism to the coke workers. It was a typical performance for him. "A sort of crusading spirit sustained many of us in those early days," he wrote. "We placed the cause of labor before personal advancement, family comfort, or anything else." In his own mind, he was a kind of latter-day apostle going out among the fishermen.

There was also the spur of competition. In 1886, when the AFL was formed, another national organization, the Noble Order of the Knights of Labor, was enjoying a meteoric rise. It had started, in 1869, as a secret organization that announced meetings by chalking strange symbols on walls and sidewalks. In 1881, in an effort to placate Catholics, who opposed its secrecy, it had become public, and, after it had won several strikes, its membership had skyrocketed. In 1886, it had some 700,000 members; the Federation claimed 316,000 but had fewer than half that number. The Noble Order, however, was not exclusively a labor organization. Its constitution barred only lawyers, bankers, doctors, and "professional" politicians. Like the National Labor Union, it swarmed with reformers, radicals, and utopians. Its leader, Terrence V. Powderly, a pink-cheeked man with a drooping white mustache, said that "to point out a way to utterly destroy the (wage) system would be a pleasure" to him. In workingmen's saloons, men sang:

> Storm the Fort, ye Knights of Labor,
> Battle for your cause,
> Equal rights for every neighbor,
> Down with tyrant laws!

But Powderly, whose title was Grand Master Workman, was, by many accounts, a confused and timid man. The thought of storming anything probably horrified him. He opposed strikes as a "relic of barbarism." He argued that wages lost in strikes would be better invested in cooperative factories. He refused to support the movement for the eight-hour day. While Sam was urging "more, more now," Powderly was advocating various panaceas, and uttering such platitudes as: "Moral wealth, not wealth, is the true standard of individual and national greatness."

After the Haymarket bombing, when Sam pleaded for clemency for the seven condemned anarchists as a matter of justice, Powderly held back. It would be "better that seven times seven men hang," he said, "than to hang the millstone of odium around the standard of this Order in affiliating in any way with this element of destruction." Sam made no effort to conceal his scorn for Powderly and for the Knights.

Nevertheless, the Knights, in bitter rivalry with Sam's "pure and simple" trade unions, often tried to capture or destroy them. Cigarmakers' Local 144 had been among the targets. The Knights' General Executive Board announced that it "had never had the pleasure of seeing Mr. Gompers sober." Sam, who prided himself on never taking a drink until the day's work was done, replied that two members of the Knights' governing body were grocery store keepers, that one was an ex-chief of the Shawnee police, and that others had been "floating like scum on the top of part of the labor movement, continually seeking to divert it to their own personal ends." About Powderly, he said: "A man in his position, who was bribed, could do the work of the employers no better."

The tone of public controversy at the time was even less courteous than it is now. During the 1884 Presidential campaign, the Democrats had chanted about the Republican candidate:

> Blaine, Blaine, James G. Blaine,
> The continental liar from the State of Maine.

The Republicans had responded with a reference to the story that the Democratic candidate, Stephen Grover Cleveland, had fathered a child out of wedlock:

> Ma! Ma. Where's my pa?
> Gone to the White House,
> Ha! Ha! Ha!

Under the circumstances, neither the attacks made on Sam nor his replies were surprising.

The rivalry with the Knights for the allegiance of workers continued all through the Federation's first years. But by the early 1890's, the Knights had disintegrated. The Federation was to have other rivals, but none that really threatened its supremacy, even briefly, until the Congress of Industrial Organizations emerged in the 1930's.

From the day that Sam assumed the presidency of the Federation, he was, as he put it, a "seeker of men," those for whom the trade union movement was "a great ideal and those who were wiling to spend and be spent in its services." His life, he said, "became an endless pilgrimage that carried [him] over the length and breadth of the country." He traveled a total of 20,000 miles in 1888. The following year, he went on a "lecture tour" of thirty-seven cities. In 1891, accompanied by McGuire, he made a tour of the anthracite coal fields in Pennsylvania. "There was not a union to be found," he wrote, "not even a secret organization. We were seeking a few men in each locality who would be willing to constitute the nucleus of a labor union." They were difficult to find. The "seeking," as Sam noted, was not a "safe undertaking." Company gunmen were thick in the anthracite fields. They thought nothing of shooting or clubbing those they regarded as labor agitators. Nevertheless, Sam and McGuire persisted until they found the men they wanted.

In 1891, Sam also made his first trip to the Pacific Coast. Like all of his trips, it was grueling. Some years earlier, Frank Leslie, publisher of *Frank Leslie's Illustrated Newspaper*, had traveled to the Pacific Coast by Pullman, and his paper had treated it as a considerable adventure. An artist's sketch showed him "dining at twenty miles an hour." "It sounds appalling," Leslie wrote, "and still more appalling were the faithful and reliable accounts of friends who had gone over these three thousand, three hundred miles before us, and followed the setting sun at the rate of twenty miles an hour." Sam didn't travel by Pullman. He made his way across the country by "immigrant trains, freight cars, and cheap boats." He found it a "soul-searing ordeal."

His trip to the Pacific Coast reflected his growing stature as a labor leader. In Denver, he was invited to address both houses of the state legislature. At a meeting in that city, he was welcomed by the mayor and by the governor of the state. In Salt Lake City, where he visited a cigar factory and displayed his skill at rolling cigars, the governor of Utah, which was then a territory, introduced him at a public meeting. When Sam reached San Francisco, members of the Coast Seamen's Union, dressed in uniforms, were lined up to greet him, and they escorted him through the streets to Shoemakers' Hall, where he spoke. Each day, when he wasn't traveling, there was a steady round of conferences, meetings, and speeches, and, at the end of each day, he sent dispatches covering the day's events to newspapers in the East. He understood, as few men of his time did, the importance of a good press. "Everywhere I went," he recalled in later years, "I tried to make friends with reporters so that labor's story might find a hearing in the daily papers."

Often, he fascinated reporters. Paul Bellamy, who later became editor of the Cleveland *Plain Dealer*, saw a good deal of Sam. Bellamy once wrote of him:

> He can say commonplace things—though he rarely does—and make them sound like the ringing periods of a new declaration of independence. If he were to go into your house this [Sunday] morning, smile at you out of his grey eyes—the color of a gun barrel—and declare: "Eggs for breakfast should never be boiled more than three minutes," you and all within the sound of his voice would immediately forget that it was Sunday and go out and organize a national party to include the principle of three-minute eggs in the federal constitution. It is impossible to isolate the germ of magnetism like that. All you can say is that some people have it—at most a few in a generation.

In San Francisco, Sam renewed his friendship with Andrew Furuseth, the sailors' leader in whom he recognized a devotion to labor's cause equal to his own. Furuseth, who went tieless and often in a frayed shirt, even when he visited the United States Senate, never accepted more than a seaman's wage from his union. When he went to sea, he traveled steerage. Sam thought him "a genius with extraordinary dramatic power" and "the spirit of a crusader." The two men, one short and squat and the other tall and gaunt, were among the most picturesque labor leaders of their time.

There was a movement to run Furuseth for Congress. Sam advised against it. "Don't waste him by sending him to Congress where he'll be a lone dissenting voice," he said. "Keep him here as your leader."

The Federation was growing. By 1890, it had approximately 250,000 members. Its annual income from per capita dues payments, which were one-quarter of a cent per member per month, was still less than $10,000 a year, but this represented a significant gain over its first-year income of $2,100. It had acquired new offices, which a visiting journalist described as "dark and dingy," but which Sam remembered fondly as consisting of "two large rooms and one small room." Previously, it had moved from its first headquarters, the shed on East Eighth Street, to the front room of the Gompers apartment. It had created difficulties; Sam's family had been all but crowded into the street. The Federation had also acquired, after "careful consideration," a secondhand typewriter for $55. Sam promptly used it to send letters urging support for the eight-hour day to the President, Cabinet members, forty senators, seventy-five representatives, and a hundred economists. Members sometimes complained that the Federation was placing too much emphasis on a single objective. "We want eight hours," Sam replied to one of them. "We are determined to have eight hours." He considered a shorter workday essential to the improvement of labor's condition. It had broad implications for him. "As we get an hour's more leisure every day," he told a United States Industrial Commission, "it means millions of golden hours, of opportunities, to the human family."

On February 22, 1889, there were meetings for the eight-hour day in 240 cities, and nearly a thousand additional meetings were held during the year. It represented a major effort. Results, however, were to be slow in coming.

Sam tried to extend the movement for the eight-hour day to Europe. A meeting of the International Workingmen's Congress was to be held in Paris in 1889, and he enlisted a seaman named Hugh McGregor, who was helping him at the Federation's office, and who was "idealist enough to recognize no practical difficulties," to serve as his courier to the congress. They scraped together enough money for his passage, and McGregor packed a few things, "including a reserve celluloid collar," into a small bag, and off he went. At the congress, the resolution for the eight-hour day was passed over the opposition of German socialist leaders Karl Liebknecht and August Bebel, and the first demonstration for it, the following year, was the beginning of the European May Day celebrations. McGregor, who thus earned himself a footnote in labor history, returned with his beard trimmed in what was then called the "Lord Dundreary style" and with a new set of false teeth, which he discarded because they made it difficult for him to smoke his corncob pipe.

The Federation's president was alternately concerned with large matters and small, with spectacular crises and the drudge work of systematically building the organization. In 1892, the Federation donated $500 to striking coal miners in Tennessee and $500 more to metal miners at Coeur d'Alene, Idaho, where a bloody strike was in progress. These amounts, though modest, represented a third of the balance in the AFL treasury at the time. An even larger effort was made in behalf of the strikers at the Carnegie Steel Company at Homestead, Pennsylvania. Carnegie, a paternalistic employer who invited his men to call him "Andy," was away in Europe. "Put all your eggs in one basket," he was fond of advising people, "and watch that basket." But he had entrusted his basket to Henry C. Frick, a notorious foe of unions. The strike was called when Frick imposed a wage reduction. He called in the Pinkerton Detective Agency, and, since entry to the plant was blocked by pickets, it was arranged to have the Pinkertons moved by barges up the Monongahela River to company property. The plan miscarried. There was a pitched battle between the Pinkertons and the strikers, which lasted for twelve hours. Three guards and seven workers were killed. Sam, with more than his customary zeal, rallied support for the strikers. There was a "Homestead Day," and union members throughout the country were asked to give part of a day's pay for the strikers. More than $7,000 was raised, but the strike was lost. Years later, Carnegie told Sam that the strike would never have occurred if he had been in this country. "No grief of my life," he said, "approaches that of Homestead." Sam noted that steel companies, including Carnegie's, made a practice of maintaining an "excessive labor force" that included many "recent immigrants hostile to unions."

Meanwhile, the flow of communications from the Federation's president often served to hold unions together and to guide them. His letters in this period reveal the common sense and painstaking patience with which he shepherded the young organization. He advised officers of the Brewery Workers' Union to shun "personalities and abuse" in a dispute with dissident locals. In a letter to the head of the Coopers' Union, he expressed "astonishment" at the use of such words as "czar and henchmen" in criticizing another union officer. He asked John Kirchner, an officer of the Cigarmakers' Union, to help form a local union of hair-spinning workers in Philadelphia. Occasionally, he was stern. When an officer of the National Horse Collar Workers' Union complained that the Federation hadn't provided adequate financial help during one of its strikes, he answered: "How much financial aid do you think, by the payment of a quarter of a cent, can be rendered to organizations whose aggregate payments (as was the case with yours) amount to from ninety-nine cents to one dollar and twenty cents?" A union officer who asked what expense would be entailed in having the Federation's president address a meeting in his community was told, "About the probable expense of the trip, let me say that you know what the fare is, and that, with a slight additional necessary expense, is all the outlay required for me." Generally, he returned from such trips out of pocket. He embarked on them with a missionary's zeal. He used them to organize local unions, to put local unions in the same trade in touch with each other, and even to solicit individual members. "The name of the American Federation of Labor is becoming a household word," he reported to the Executive Council after one trip. "I believe I have succeeded in arousing a general interest in its methods, and in making its objects known in a most effective manner. I have found the unions full of enthusiasm for our common cause."

# 8

## "More, More Now"

"Somehow," Sam noted with satisfaction, "the Federation was struggling along, gaining a bit month by month." His own unrelenting efforts, he knew, were a major factor in this progress. It inspired an almost paternal pride in him. He was devoted to his wife, Sophia, and to their children, but it was the Federation that absorbed him. The needs of his family were less compelling to him than those of the miners, musicians, brewery workers, and workers in dozens of other trades and industries whose future, he felt, had been entrusted to his hands. Over the years, he was to have a part in organizing twenty-eight national unions. In 1893, however, the Federation's progress bumped to a halt as the second major economic crisis and depression in Sam's American experience swept across the country.

The year was to have several claims on history. In Oklahoma, the Cherokee Strip, one of the last remnants of the frontier, was opened to a frenzied dash by land-hungry homesteaders. In Chicago, the Columbia Exposition was electrifying the country with a Ferris wheel 250 feet high, which dwarfed most urban structures, and with an Egyptian Village where American girls, made up as Egyptians, did "hootchy-kootchy" dances. The dances, said one viewer, "pleased men of simple carnal minds whether they came from Boston, Oshkosh, or Kalamazoo." But it was the depression, which put more than three million men out of work, that filled Sam's mind. He thought it "brutally stupid" in a country "as big and fertile as ours."

By 1893, the thirteen colonies had evolved into a nation of more than sixty-three million people. In 1890, the Fifty-first Congress had become the first to vote a billion-dollar budget. When it was taunted as a "Billion-Dollar Congress," the Republican Speaker of the House, Thomas Brackett Reed, replied: "Yes, but this is a billion-dollar country." The national wealth in that year was actually estimated at more than sixty billion. The United States had already far surpassed Germany, Great Britain, and France. But prosperity was still limited to the very few. Even before the depression struck, around eleven million of the country's twelve million families were living on incomes of less than $400 a year. Hamlin Garland, the novelist, returned to his home in Osage, Iowa, after an absence of six years to find that every home he visited "had its individual message of sordid struggle and half-hidden despair. Of such pain and futility are the lives of the average man and woman of both city and country composed," he told himself. "Why lie about it?"

In Barry, Illinois, on Christmas Eve, a six-year-old boy named Floyd Dell, who would grow up to become a novelist, was startled when his parents pretended not to know that the next day was Christmas. He crawled numbly into bed "as if I had been hit by something," he recalled years later. "It was hard to breathe. I ached all through. I was stunned with finding out the truth. We're poor," he whispered to himself. "We're poor."

In Chicago, where the AFL held its annual convention in December, the "pain and futility" Garland had observed and the poverty that had numbed young Floyd Dell were unavoidably plain. Hundreds of homeless men sought refuge from the

This is how a cartoonist for the *Utica Globe*
saw Gompers' analysis of men's ambitions.

winter cold in the corridors and on the staircases of the convention hall. "We had to walk down the stairs very carefully," Sam wrote, "for we had to pick our way over the men who were lying on the steps and on the floors with only newspapers for covering. It was a scene that burned into my mind." He could understand such suffering, he said, when it resulted from flood or blight; it outraged him when people had to endure hunger because there were no jobs for them.

Earlier in the year, he had tried to get the governor of New York to help that state's unemployed. The governor, a banker, had declined. At Sam's suggestion, New York City unions then staged a meeting at Madison Square Garden to protest the government's indifference. The unionists, many of them unemployed, crowded the huge hall, and feelings ran high. As was often the case in the days before amplifiers, most of the speakers could not be heard. But Sam's big voice filled the hall. It was not his usual speech; it was a harangue. As he looked out over the immense audience, many of them hungry, his feelings were so "agonized," he said, that he would not have "hesitated entering into any undertaking that would bring about a radical change and make amends for a state so horrid in a country of intelligence and civilization." He had not felt that way since the harsh experience of seeing his family go hungry when, after the cigarmakers' strike in 1877, he had been blacklisted. At the meeting, "in the bitterness of his soul," he recited:

> Oh, that a poor man's son as has been said,
> Became a convict to earn his bread,
> That a poor man's daughter to earn a crust,
> Became a victim of some rich man's lust.
> Oh, angels shut thine eyes,
> Let conflagration illumine the outraged skies!
> Let red Nemesis burn the hellish clan,
> And chaos end the slavery of man!

It was an extraordinary speech from the president of the American Federation of Labor, a man already famous—or infamous, from the radicals' point of view—for his prudence. The audience came to its feet in wild cheering when he finished. He could have led it into any action. But he quickly realized that he had been guilty of a failing he often attributed to his radical critics. He had allowed passion to dominate intellect. Instead of advocating constructive action, he had simply appealed to the emotions of his audience. His old mentor, Laurrell, would have frowned in disapproval. Sam himself was abashed. "The responsibility of my utterance haunted me," he wrote, "not only that night but for many a day after."

At the Federation's Chicago convention, he was still "seething against injustice," but he was under control. He indulged in no harangues. He saw the depression as a conclusive argument for the eight-hour day. A shorter workday would mean more jobs. "A practical, just, and safe equilibrium can be maintained in an industrial world for the fast and ever-increasing introduction of machinery by a commensurate reduction of the hours of labor," he said. He wanted "a guarantee that employment, remunerative and healthful," would be made available to all. He neglected to say how this could be given. Socialists at the convention presented a resolution calling for collective ownership and operation of industry as a solution to the country's economic problems. Actually, it was plank 10 of an omnibus resolution advocating numerous reforms. Sam, of course, was opposed to plank 10. He was opposed to any effort to commit the Federation to a theory for transforming society. "I am entirely at variance with your philosophy," he told the Socialists at one convention. "Economically, you are unsound; socially, you are wrong; industrially, you are an impossibility."

He refused to recognize the revolutionary implications of his own credo: "More, more now, more tomorrow." In 1914, he was to have an interesting exchange with a Socialist leader, Morris Hillquit, on this point. Hillquit was a soft-voiced and brilliant lawyer. He respected the function of trade unions and served a number of them, but he thought them too limited in their goals. Parts of the exchange are worth recording.

MR. HILLQUIT: Then one of the functions of organized labor is to increase the share of the workers in the product of their labor. Is that correct?

MR. GOMPERS: Yes, sir. Organized labor makes constantly increasing demand upon society for reward for the services which the workers render to society, and without which civilized life would be impossible.

MR. HILLQUIT: And these demands for an increasing share of the product of labor continue as a gradual process all the time?

MR. GOMPERS: I am not so sure as to gradual process. Sometimes it is not a gradual process, but it is all the time.

MR. HILLQUIT: All the time?

MR. GOMPERS: Yes, sir. . . . The aim is to secure the best conditions obtainable for the workers.

MR. HILLQUIT: Yes, and when these conditions are obtained——

MR. GOMPERS (interrupting): Why then we want better——

MR. HILLQUIT (continuing): You will strive for better?

MR. GOMPERS: Yes.

MR. HILLQUIT: Now, my question is, will this effort on the part of organized labor ever stop before the workers receive the full reward for their labor?

MR. GOMPERS: It won't stop at all at any particular point, whether it be that towards which you have just stated, or anything else. The working people will never stop in their effort to obtain a better life for themselves, and for their wives and for their children and for humanity.

MR. HILLQUIT: Then the object of the organized workmen is to obtain complete social justice for themselves and for their wives and for their children?

MR. GOMPERS: It is the effort to obtain a better life every day.

MR. HILLQUIT: Every day, and always——

MR. GOMPERS (interrupting): Every day. That does not limit it.

MR. HILLQUIT: Until such time——

MR. GOMPERS (interrupting): Not until any time.

MR. HILLQUIT: In other words——

MR. GOMPERS (interrupting): In other words, we go farther than you. You have an end; we have not.

"Theoretically," Hillquit commented, "the close kinship of aims and interests between the socialist and trade union movements was thus once more strikingly established." Sam refused to acknowledge it. The logic was with Hillquit, as Sam probably realized, but he didn't want the labor movement put in the strait jacket of theory.

The 1893 depression, several months old when the delegates assembled in Chicago, was, in a sense, the first major test of the young organization. Previous depressions had invariably meant disaster for what there had been of an American labor movement. But, as Sam was able to report to the convention: "The unions now in existence have manifested, not only the powers of resistance, but of stability and permanency. This fact in itself is the best answer to all trade union antagonists, carping critics, and sophists." Later, he wrote to a friend that he was "elated by the manner in which we have withstood [the depression's] fearful effects." He predicted confidently that the Federation's policies would, with the revival of industry, "give an impetus to our movement unparalleled in American history." But there would be shoals to navigate before clear water was reached.

In June, 1893, the American Railway Union (ARU) had been organized as an industrial union, in competition with existing railway unions. Eugene Victor Debs, an evangelical locomotive fireman from Terre Haute, Indiana, became its president. Debs had been editor of the publication of the Brotherhood of Locomotive Firemen, and Sam, although he respected Debs's idealism, was "shocked" by his action. He was always shocked when men "tried to fit the labor movement into a different shape from that into which it had naturally developed. It is hard for the reformer," he observed sadly, "to realize that the labor movement is a living thing, and that it must develop by passing through the normal stages of growth." Sam believed that craft unions, which united men on the basis of their skills, represented one of these normal stages. He had not, however, shut his eyes to the possibility of change. At the Federation's convention in 1888, he had suggested that it might become desirable to bring craft unions together in industrial divisions. Debs was less patient. He thought that the ARU, as an industrial union, would have "superior advantages" that would enable it to "absorb" the other unions of railroad workers.

Unfortunately for his new organization, the ARU soon became engaged in an unequal contest. Late in 1893, as the depression deepened, the Pullman Palace Car Company, in Illinois, cut the wages of its workers by 20 per cent or more. The workers lived in a company-owned town outside of Chicago, where they had to pay exorbitant prices for everything from rent to water, but George Pullman, the inventor of the Pullman car and owner of the company, saw fit not to reduce these prices along with wages. He was an autocrat. He fired members of a workers' committee who tried to get him to listen to their grievances. He rejected proposals for arbitration. "We have nothing to arbitrate," he announced. "The workers have nothing to do with the amount of wages they shall receive." "A man who won't meet his men halfway is a God-damn fool," exclaimed Mark Hanna, the national Republican boss and one of the country's leading industrialists. But Pullman's attitude was the prevailing one.

In 1894, his workers struck, and the ARU, which had advised against the strike, assumed direction of it. A sympathetic boycott of all trains carrying Pullman cars was organized. By July, all railroad traffic into Chicago had been halted. But, by then, a familiar story had unfolded. A federal court had issued an injunction prohibiting railroad employees from interfering with the mails or with interstate commerce. President Cleveland ordered U.S. marshals and troops into Chicago to enforce it. Sam protested the use of troops, as did Illinois governor John P. Altgeld. Cleveland was unmoved. "If it takes the entire army and navy of the United States to deliver a postal card into Chicago," he proclaimed, "that postal card will be delivered."

It would have been absurd to expect any other policy from Cleveland. He was a conservative of a kind unknown today. In vetoing a bill to provide seeds in areas stricken by drought, he had said that he saw no reason "to indulge a benevolent and charitable sentiment through the appropriation of public funds for that purpose."

Pullman's unfeeling arrogance, and Cleveland's obvious determination to crush the strike, aroused furious emotions in union men throughout the country. Sam had watched the situation developing in Chicago with a goading sense of helplessness. He had no great fondness for the heads of the railroad craft unions whom Debs was challenging. The Brotherhood of Locomotive Firemen, whose publication Debs had once edited, had been denied admission by the Federation when it had refused to drop a constitutional provision limiting membership to whites. Naturally, Sam detested everything that Pullman represented. But he saw nothing that he could do.

On July 9, he received a telegram from Chicago trade union representatives asking him to come to Chicago "immediately" and call a general strike. Actually, as he sometimes told audiences, he had no authority to call a strike of any kind. That could be done only by individual unions. Furthermore, he had no illusions that a general strike could succeed even under favorable circumstances. In the midst of a depression, it would be a hopeless venture. Nevertheless, he wired members of the Federation's Executive Council and the leaders of national unions to confer with him in Chicago on July 12. After listening to Debs and other union representatives, they wired an appeal to Cleveland to use his influence "so that the present industrial crisis may be brought to an end, alike to the advantage of the people of our country and the institutions under which we live." The President ignored it.

Short of urging a general strike, which Sam opposed on the grounds that it could "easily destroy" the labor movement, there was little the Federation could do. It is worth noting that James R. Sovereign, who had succeeded Powderly as Grand Master Workman of the Knights of Labor, did issue a call for a general strike by his own organization. There was no response. A cartoon in a Chicago newspaper depicted him as a latter-day King Canute enthroned by the sea and ordering the waves to stop. It was a role for which Sam had no taste.

The Pullman strike was broken, and the American Railway

Union with it. Debs was sentenced to a year in jail for violating the federal injunction. He was to emerge an eloquent spokesman for American socialism and a tragic-heroic figure in American life.

The Federation's Executive Council, in Chicago, had issued an appeal to workers to use their votes, as "American freemen," to "redeem this country from its present political and industrial misrule." After the fall elections, in which the Democratic Party fared badly, Sam wired Cleveland:

> Without much concert of effort by organized labor, the people have answered at the polls your assumption of an unconstitutional and unwarrantable use of the military power to crush labor. Though the change may benefit us little, the rebuke will nevertheless be appreciated and remembered.

It was perhaps indiscreet, but Sam felt that basic constitutional rights had been violated. Such violations never failed to incense him.

# 9

## *Defeat and Victory*

In 1894, Sam was forty-four years old. Strands of gray were showing in his hair, his lush mustache, and the tuft of beard he wore immediately beneath his lower lip. The devil-may-care look had disappeared from his face. Eight years in the presidency of the Federation, with its exhausting demands, had taken their toll. There was a certain sobriety in his appearance. But the immigrant boy, who had started work at the age of ten, had established himself as the country's pre-eminent labor leader. His position, however, was being increasingly challenged. In 1890, a Socialist trade unionist, T. J. Morgan, had opposed Sam, but Morgan had had little support. In 1891, Sam had had two opponents but had again been elected by an overwhelming majority. In 1893, however, he had faced a real threat from John T. McBride, president of the United Mine Workers and a man with considerable political experience. McBride had been a member of the Ohio legislature and a candidate for Secretary of State. Peter McGuire had also been nominated for the presidency; he had withdrawn in favor of McBride. Some, firmly in

Art Young, a brilliant radical cartoonist, saw the AFL president as holding the lid down on the militancy of the American labor movement. (Bettman Archives)

Sam's camp in the past, had voted for McBride, but Sam had won by ninety-two votes. The fact that the presidency, as well as other offices, was now being contested was symptomatic of the Federation's growing strength, income, and prestige. In earlier years, delegates had to be persuaded to accept office. The presidency, as Sam had noted, had carried with it little money and no honor, and had been coveted by no one. That had now changed.

In 1894, when the Federation convened in Denver, McBride was again a candidate. The continuing depression had thinned the number of delegates, and the United Mine Workers, according to Sam, had inflated its membership to gain votes. It was a contentious convention. The Socialists' plank 10 was again up for debate. Sam's irreconcilable opposition to the Socialists did not endear him to them; they joined with McBride's supporters. As a result, Sam was defeated by a vote of 1,170 to 976. The convention also decided to move the Federation's headquarters from New York to Indianapolis, which Sam had opposed, but it elected him, perhaps as a consolation prize, a fraternal delegate to the 1895 British Trade Union Congress. Sam later made light of his defeat. He referred to it as his "sabbatical year." "A great weight seemed to roll from my shoulders," he wrote. Nevertheless, it was a hard blow for him. To a very great degree, the Federation had been his creation. Now, it had rejected him.

One man was especially delighted by Sam's humbling. Daniel DeLeon, a small, handsome, Venezuelan-born Jew with flashing eyes and a dark, pointed beard, detested everything that Sam represented. DeLeon had been educated in Germany and at Columbia University, where he subsequently taught, and his first foray into politics had been as a single-taxer. Around 1890, he joined the Socialist Labor Party. He soon established himself as a leader of the most doctrinaire sort, intolerant of views deviating from his own, and full of invective for his opponents. It was he who first denounced Sam as a "labor fakir" and as a "greasy tool of Wall Street." Sam's "pure and simple" trade unions were "pure and simpledom" to DeLeon. He was against "everything less than the abolition of wage slavery." He thought improvements in working conditions were "gains for capitalism" and "only a kind of cheap whiskey" for the workers. (Some radical intellectuals still cling to this view. "To work for the improvement of the existing democracy," Professor Herbert Marcuse says in *An Essay on Liberation*, "appears as indefinitely delaying attainment of the goal of creating a free society.")

DeLeon and his followers had worked against Sam at the

1894 convention. No doubt, he hoped that he would be able to capture the Federation. It was not to be. His life was one of endless frustration. He tried unsuccessfully to capture the remains of the Knights of Labor. He split the Socialist Labor Party by expelling everyone who resisted his orthodoxy. He established his own Socialist Trades and Labor Alliance; it was highly centralized, organized on industrial lines, and appealed to workers to "strike against the capitalist system" by supporting the Socialist Labor Party. His obsession with doctrine suggested Samuel Butler's couplet:

> Petulant, capricious sects,
> Maggots of corrupted texts.

DeLeon, probably more than any other man, had a capacity for getting under Sam's skin. The working people had "no more dangerous enemy," Sam wrote, than those who, "under the mask of sympathy with the toiler struggling for justice," pretended to have an "immediate and absolute remedy" for all of their ills. He could not match DeLeon's invective. Friends advised him that it was a waste of time to reply to his critic; Sam found his irritation difficult to contain. "There is not a charge or insinuation which the skinflint employer, corporation thug or apologist, or villainous newspaper penny-a-liner had launched against labor organizations," he wrote in the *Federationist*, "that this *agent provocateur* has not rehashed, embellished, and served up just at the time when it will serve the interests of the capitalist class best." He was too wordy.

Sam said that, after his defeat, he thought of returning to the cigarmaker's bench, where he had "enjoyed life so much." That is improbable. Since 1881, when he had gone to Pittsburgh as a delegate to the conference that had established the Federation of Organized Trades and Labor Unions, he had felt immersed in great events. Apart from his total commitment to labor's cause, there is no doubt that he enjoyed being a mover and shaker. It is difficult to believe that he gave any serious thought to retiring into the obscurity of a cigar factory.

In any event, everything he did showed that he was determined to continue influencing events. He wrote, he lectured, he undertook to help organize for the United Garment Workers, and he journeyed through the South for them.

"The trip constituted my first real acquaintance with the South," he wrote. It made him "realize the difference between racial problems as theories and practical solutions." In 1891, the Federation had convened in Birmingham, and had changed hotels to get decent treatment for its several Negro delegates. By a vote of fifty-one to three, the convention had adopted a resolution rebuking unions that "exclude from membership persons on account of race or color." A year earlier, Sam had said: "Our employers care very little for what we are as long as we work cheap." He favored "encouraging the recognition of equality [in economic opportunity] between colored and white laborers." He believed that the Federation should give Negroes "every assistance." Later, he would assign organizers to provide such assistance. He would express pride in New Orleans trade unionists when they declared a general strike in sympathy with Negro draymen. Testifying before the U.S. Industrial Commission in 1899, he would say:

> Organized labor of New Orleans went on a strike; every machinist went on a strike; every printer went on a strike; no paper made its appearance; the men working in the gas houses went on a strike and there was no illumination that night; the bakers went on a strike, and all other white workers went on a strike for the purpose of securing recognition of the colored workmen.

Sam, however, would never become an advocate of social equality for Negroes. Perhaps his southern trip had persuaded him that it would be an unacceptable view at the time. Perhaps he was not entirely immune to the prevailing prejudices.

In late August, he and McGuire, who had also been elected

a fraternal delegate to the British Trade Union Congress, embarked for England. The Federation had voted Sam $225 for his passage, expenses, and compensation. He traveled second-class, but it was a triumphant journey. In London, he paid a nostalgic visit to his old home on Fort Street. Many of his relatives and old neighbors were still living in the vicinity. He had left thirty-two years earlier as an apprentice cigarmaker; he returned as an important figure. He would have been less than human if he had not enjoyed the transformation. After London, he and McGuire went to Paris, Hamburg, and Amsterdam, where they met with labor and political leaders. He had acquired many European friends, including Paul Deschanel, who was to become President of the French Republic, and, one gathers, he was warmly received.

Meanwhile, back in the United States, affairs were going well for him. Sam always insisted that he had never sought office of any kind. The office had always sought him, he said. He did not object, apparently, when others sought office for him. His close friend George W. Perkins, President of the Cigarmakers' International Union, had busied himself lining up delegates for Sam for the next Federation convention. "If you can show to a number of delegates that, in the interests of our cause, they ought to vote for me," Sam wrote, "I am sure that you will do so, and I shall appreciate your action beyond measure. Heretofore, I even forbade that but now I can see my error, especially in view of what I am informed McB is doing."

"McB," of course, was McBride. His handling of the Federation presidency could not have been better calculated to pave the way for Sam's return. Sam had respected the limited authority of his office. The Federation had always been for him "a voluntary banding together of autonomous unions" for "mutual service and welfare." He had labored mightily to win the cooperation of its affiliated unions and to reconcile differences among them. He had cajoled and persuaded; he had never presumed to dictate. McBride tended to be authoritarian in his management of the Federation's affairs, and he did not mind offending people. He told the officer of one union that certain facts existed only in his "distorted brain." He told another that a protest he had made had "simply exposed your ignorance as an official and . . . your boorishness as a man." Such behavior was not calculated to win friends and adherents.

In addition, McBride took sick, and, without bothering to get the approval of the Federation's Executive Council, he appointed one of his supporters, James Duncan, the Federation's second vice-president, to serve for him. John B. Lennon, a member of the Executive Council, found it "hard to believe." There was more.

The Federation was on record as opposing compulsory arbitration. Some of McBride's associates were distressed to find an article by him in the New York *World* endorsing it. He acted less like the head of a democratic federation of trade unions than like a potentate. Even so, at the 1895 convention, in New York City, he came close to retaining the Federation's presidency. Sam was elected by only eighteen votes. However, he was never to be successfully challenged again.

During his "sabbatical year," he said, he had been better off financially, and he had been able to spend more time with his family. In his autobiography, he suggests that he was reluctant to resume the office, and that he yielded only to pressure from his associates. Perhaps it was true; at worst, it was a pardonable deception.

The Federation's office, Sam found, when he got to Indianapolis, was "a shambles." McBride, for all his virtues, he noted sourly, "shrank from hard work." But before Sam managed to do very much to restore order, he fell sick. His illness was serious enough for Sophia to come out from New York to nurse him. The news alarmed his friends all across the country. One of them, a seaman named John F. O'Sullivan, wrote: "If you are about to peg out, you should do it quickly, turn up your toes, and not keep an anxious public waiting to hear of

your finality. Good luck and recover quickly . . . believe me
to be your beloved and dutiful son."

It is noteworthy that between Sam, a Jew, and the Irish, who
were the most influential national group in the Federation, there
was a strong affection and loyalty. In times of trouble, they
were his stoutest supporters. But then, Sam made little of his
Jewishness. "You say that it is your chief glory that you are a
Jew," he wrote to one of his coreligionists. "Mine is that I
have a heart, a mind, and a conscience, that I have struggled
with my fellow men and yearn to struggle for a better day
when the ridiculous divisions, questions which make man an
enemy to man instead of a brother, shall be eliminated." He
had little regard for organized religion generally. He thought
it "too craven to save cities, and too subservient to wealth." In
a letter to one minister, he wrote that the church talks "only
about life to come—trade unions alone can save."

# 10

## "Hurrah for William"

"Trade unions alone can save." Sam saw no salvation for workers in any other institution or movement. Just as he scoffed at
the church, he scoffed at reformers and revolutionists who
were constantly urging workers to place their hopes in political
parties. "Beware of demagoguery, especially political partyism,"
Professor Richard T. Ely, of Johns Hopkins University, had
warned workers in 1886. "[It] will give you illusory triumphs,
but leave to you only wretched failure." That was Sam's view.
Besides, he didn't want to see the Federation torn by political
quarrels. The nineteenth century, he noted, was littered with
"the wrecks of promising labor organizations, destroyed by the
disrupting wrangles of politics and zeal for office holding." At
the Federation's convention in St. Louis, Missouri, in 1888,
there was considerable sentiment for the formation by labor
of an independent political party. "It would be in the extreme
unwise," Sam said.

He was not, however, blind to the value of political action.
As president of Cigarmakers' Local 144, he had frequently

taken a boat up the Hudson River to the state capital at Albany
to lobby for legislation; he had traveled to Washington for
the same purpose. On his first visit to Washington, he had
presented the case for the eight-hour workday to President
Grant. "You are not a very tall man, Mr. Gompers," Grant had
said irrelevantly. Sam had looked across at Grant, whose
slouching posture made him seem not much taller than Sam,
and replied: "But I am not the President of the United States."
Generally, political leaders seemed tall to Sam only in their
promises. He recognized the need for the "cooperation of organized labor at the ballot box as well as in the factory, field,
and mine." But "we should rather be a unit in our demands
than a political party," he told his followers.

Essentially, this policy of remaining independent of political
parties is still followed by organized labor in the United States.
In European countries, unions have tended to ally themselves
with radical parties of one sort or another. Their rhetoric has
been far more revolutionary than that of unions in the United
States; their achievements have been significantly less. But, in
the 1880's and for nearly half a century, many people regarded
Sam's policy as reactionary. "Reform parties," he wrote, "because they had humanitarian purposes, felt that they had a
claim on the labor movement that should take precedence over
economic ends." He rejected this claim.

However, in 1896, when Sam returned to the presidency of
the Federation, the political climate in the country was changing. A reform movement, born mainly of discontent among
the farmers, was gathering force. For a time, it made his attitude
toward politics seem stubbornly perverse.

By the early 1890's, many of the homesteaders who had
rushed westward after the Civil War had the sour taste of defeat in their mouths. Many of them had simply given up. In
1891 alone, some eighteen thousand "prairie schooners" had
headed eastward across the Missouri River. More than a quarter of the country's farmers were struggling to meet payments

on high-interest mortgages. When they had bumper crops, prices fell. Periodic droughts left them penniless and in debt. It seemed to many of them that they were enslaved by the banks, which held their mortgages, and by the railroads on which they depended to transport their crops. Mary Elizabeth Pease, who was called the "Kansas Pythoness," suggested the farmers "raise less corn and more hell." Farmers elsewhere summed up their misery in one pungent sentence: "The makers of clothes are underfed; the makers of food are underclad."

Out of this discontent, which swept across rural America, came the Populist Party. The Populists wanted federal owner-ship of transportation and a graduated income tax, but their chief target was the gold standard. They wanted free coinage of silver, which had been restricted; they believed that this would favor the debtor class against the creditor class. The Populists, like the urban radicals, thought they saw simple "push-button" solutions to their complex economic problems. However, unlike the urban radicals, who were generally lead-ers without followers, the Populists spoke for legions of the discontented. In 1892, in alliance with the Knights of Labor, they ran James B. Weaver for President, and polled more than a million votes. The battle was really joined in 1894 when the Democrats in Congress, many of them with Populist sympathies, managed to enact a 2 per cent income tax on incomes of $4,000 and more. One Congressman, David A. DeArmond, had pre-dicted that passage of the tax bill would "mark the dawn of a brighter day, with more sunshine, more of the song of birds, more of that sweetest music, the laughter of children well-fed, well-clothed, and well-housed." But the Supreme Court agreed with those who saw the tax as "an assault upon capital . . . a war of the poor against the rich," and declared it unconstitu-tional.

"America is good enough for me," said J. P. Morgan, the country's most powerful financier, and William Jennings Bryan, an eloquent Populist from Nebraska who was known as the

"Boy Orator of the Platte," commented: "Whenever he doesn't like it, he can give it back to us." In 1896, Bryan tried to take it back as the Democratic candidate for President. He was nominated after his famous "cross of gold" speech at the Democratic convention in the Chicago coliseum had whipped the twenty thousand people there into a frenzy of enthusiasm. Assailing the gold standard, which had become the hated symbol of Wall Street, he intoned, "You shall not press down upon the brow of labor this crown of thorns. You shall not crucify mankind upon a cross of gold." Sam, who was in Chicago at the time, thought that Bryan "spoke the language of humanity and as the proclaimed savior of the common people."

He favored Bryan over the Republican candidate, William McKinley, but he carefully refrained from involving the Federation with the Democratic Party. Sam's policy was not an easy one to follow in 1896. Bryan courted him and the "labor vote," and the campaign, as it developed, seemed to become something very close to a confrontation between the people and the "interests." In that sense, it was a repetition of what had happened during the Henry George campaign in New York ten years earlier. "One of the most important duties of government," said Bryan, "is to put rings in the noses of hogs." The contest, said the editor of *Harper's Weekly*, was one between the "dreams and fantasies of Karl Marx" and the "true Americanism" of the Republican Party. "Probably no man in civil life," observed the *Nation*, "has succeeded in inspiring so much terror, without taking life, as Bryan." There was "a greater tenseness of feeling," Sam thought, than in any campaign in his memory. But he saw the issue of free silver versus the gold standard as a "middle class" affair that would "simply divert attention from the [workers'] own interests." He wrote to Ben Tillet, the British labor leader, that, since both candidates are "blessed with the same Christian name, I cannot be charged with being partisan if I shout, 'Hurrah for William.' " He was not that indifferent. He was to vote for Bryan in 1896, 1900, and 1908.

On Labor Day, Sam spoke at Danville, Illinois, then went to Chicago to attend a dinner. Bryan, who was present as a guest, announced that, if he were elected, he would name Sam to his Cabinet. Sam replied that, although he hoped for Bryan's election, "no circumstance" could persuade him to accept a Cabinet post or any other office. It was not the first time that he had rejected the idea of a political career. In 1889, he had been nominated for the New York State Senate by the Republicans and by a powerful faction within the Democratic Party. His election had been all but assured; he had refused to become a candidate. Five years later, the Republicans had offered to run him for Congress. Again, he had declined.

Sam had never had any party entanglements; he refused to acquire any. He had cast his first vote for Grant, in 1872, because it had seemed to him that the Republicans then still represented the ideals of freedom for which the Civil War had been fought. Grant's Democratic opponent was Horace Greeley, a liberal and an outspoken friend of labor, whom Sam admired, but the Democratic Party was dominated by an alliance of Southern Bourbons and New York's Boss Tweed and other corrupt political bosses. Sam's loyalty to the Republicans had dissolved during the panic of 1873; he had formed no new ones. He had supported Peter Cooper, the patron of Cooper Union, in 1876, and Weaver, the Populist, in 1880 and again in 1892. He and Weaver had become friends. He later helped Weaver in gaining statehood for the Territory of Oklahoma. At the convention in which the constitution for the new state was written, the pen with which it was signed was presented to Sam. In another tribute to him, the new state adopted as its emblem the clasped hands of the Federation emblem. The emblem had probably been inspired by the Hand-in-Hand Society, a Hebrew mutual aid group in which Sam held membership. He had an intense interest in politics. But he had no desire, as an individual, to associate himself with any political party; as president of the Federation, he thought it would be ruinous.

Trade unions, he told the Federation convention in 1896, "are the business organizations of the wage earners." It was their business "to secure for the toilers relief from the long hours of burdensome toil, and find work for those who cannot find work at all, to fight for the full enfranchisement of labor, not only at the polls, in the halls of legislation, but far more important than all these, in the factory workshop and mine." Sam's description of unions as "the business organizations of wage earners" has suggested to some people that he had a narrow, an excessively materialistic, view of their mission. He saw broad, humanitarian implications in what he was doing. The emphasis on economic gains and the democratization of the workshop was, as he saw it, the surest way "to raise man and woman from the sloughs of poverty and despair to a proper appreciation of their rights and duties." This mission, he told his followers, "is worthy of our best efforts, our highest aspirations, our noblest impulses."

He was interested in politics mainly to the extent that politics could be used to advance the cause of labor. The Federation, now ten years old, was firmly established, he noted. It had two stenographers, a typist, a shipping clerk, and an office boy. It had withstood the attacks of the Knights of Labor, which had disintegrated; it had withstood the more serious onslaught of financial crisis and depression. The ferocity of the 1896 campaign had troubled him. He urged Federation unions "to exercise care in the expressions of our declarations, so that our motives and purposes may not be misunderstood by friends or foes. [We must distinguish], he said, "between the consciousness of our rights and hatred of others." More than ever, he wanted the Federation not to be enticed into partisan politics. His views of what constituted partisanship would change.

# II

## *An Infuriating Period*

The Federation moved its headquarters to Washington the following year, which pleased Sam immensely. He didn't care for Indianapolis. It was too far removed from his Eastern friends, and, besides, he probably associated it with his defeat in 1894. He moved his family into a modest row house there, and went on with his work.

After the 1894 convention, a group of Boston labor men had given a breakfast in Sam's honor. They had presented him with a set of books by Herbert Spencer, the English philosopher who was then enjoying a considerable vogue in the United States. Sam was fascinated by a phrase in one of Spencer's books. It read, "From the indefinite and incoherent heterogeneity to the definite coherent homogeneity." It seemed to summarize what he had been trying to accomplish in the labor movement. He was trying to weld the scattered elements of labor, often at war with one another, into a united legion that would be able to advance against its corporate enemies. But that goal was far from being achieved. In 1897, he had to contend with another of a long series of disputes within the labor movement. The Western Federation of Miners, headed by a man named Edward Boyce, threatened to disaffiliate from the Federation. Boyce said to Sam that "the men of the West are 100 years ahead of their brothers in the East" and that he wasn't really a trade unionist, anyway. He wanted, he said, "to get out and fight with the sword or use the ballot with intelligence." Extreme militancy was natural for the metal miners. In nearly every strike, they had to contend with armed vigilantes or with local deputies and the National Guard called in to do the bidding of the mine owners. Sam rejected the use of violence. "Force may have changed forms of government," he told Boyce, but it has "never attained liberty." He did his best to persuade the mine workers' leader to stay within the Federation. Boyce, however, was marching to a different cadence. He established the Western Labor Union as a rival to the Federation; it attracted few supporters. A few years later, he "struck it rich" as a prospector, and lost interest in fighting labor's battles with a sword or anything else. Sam had told him that labor's progress depended on its readiness to persevere "manfully, heroically, and with self-sacrifice." Boyce obviously preferred an easier life. He was not the first, nor would he be the last, of Sam's critics to abandon the battle.

A battle—or rather a war—of another sort broke out in 1898. On the night of February 15, in the Havana harbor, the *Maine*, a small U.S. battleship, bew up. Two hundred and sixty-six officers and crewmen died in the disaster. Immediately, the *New York Journal* and the *World*, competing yellow journals at the time, began to whip up a war hysteria. The *Journal*, under the front-page headline "DESTRUCTION OF THE WARSHIP MAINE WAS THE WORK OF AN ENEMY," ran an elaborate diagram purporting to show how a submarine mine could have been used to blow up the ship. Actually, there was no proof that this had happened. But such matters, no doubt, were good for circulation. One newspaper cartoon showed Spain as a piratical ape gloating over the multilated bodies of American sailors. Mark Hanna and other industrialists influential in the Republican Party didn't want the country dragged into a war with Spain. Business was climbing out of the depression; war might send it down into the depths again. President McKinley tried to quiet the newspapers. But the jingoists were in full cry. "McKinley," said Theodore Roosevelt, then Assistant Secretary of the Navy, "has no more backbone than a chocolate eclair." TR was in a rage. For more than seven weeks, McKinley temporized. Then, on April 11, against his better judgment, he asked Congress to declare war on Spain "in the name of humanity, in the name of civilization, in behalf of endangered American interests."

Sam's feelings were mixed. He had helped Cuban revolutionary groups based in New York; he wanted to see Cuba rid of Spanish domination. But he thought of himself as a "pronounced pacifist." Workers are always "required to bear the brunt of the battle," he had told the *World* in 1897. "It is therefore more essential to them than to all others that international disputes should be settled by arbitration instead of by force of arms." The wave of imperialist emotion touched off in the United States by the war appalled him.

The war with Spain ended in August. American battle casualties had been relatively light. Full of swagger, the *Journal* ran a banner headline: "HOW DO YOU LIKE THE JOURNAL'S WAR?" It wasn't only the *Journal*. In London, American Ambassador John Hay, who had been so distressed by the violence of strikers in Ohio some twenty years earlier, wrote to Roosevelt: "It has been a splendid little war." In Kansas, William Allen White, who was gaining prominence as editor of the *Emporia Gazette*, wrote: "Only Anglo-Saxons can govern themselves. . . . It is the Anglo-Saxons' manifest destiny to go forth as world conquerors. . . . This is what fate holds for the chosen people." In Chicago, Sam asked a peace jubilee: "Where is the spirit of holding out the helping hand in aid of all people struggling for liberty and independence? Is it not strange that now, for the first time, we hear that Cubans are unfit for self-government; that whether they protest against it or not, they must be dominated by us, annexed to us, or become a dependency of ours?"

He was not taken in by the superpatriots who wanted to see his country extend its dominion. "Citizenship in a great and powerful country is something to be proud of," he wrote, "but being great and powerful, it behooves us to do what we can that we may use that power with discretion and in the interests of right and humanity, not unnecessarily pick quarrels with people of other nations."

It was, in some respects, a most infuriating period. "Pure and enlightened womanhood" was on a rampage, as one historian has noted, and even such words as "belly," "damn," and "vomit" were considered offensive to a woman's eyes. But beneath the veneer of gentility, the country was quite different. "I have been reading the morning newspaper," Mark Twain wrote to William Dean Howells, "well knowing that I shall find in it the usual depravities and baseness and hypocrisies and cruelties that make up civilization, and cause me to put in the rest of the day pleading for the damnation of the human race."

Sam never succumbed to such morbid gloom. There was nothing of the pessimist in him. He was too busy changing the world. But personal tragedy scarred him in 1898. He was speaking in Des Moines, Iowa, during an organizing tour, when he was handed a telegram notifying him that Rose, the older of his two daughters, had died. The news shook him. "Mother and I," he wrote in his autobiography, "had buried many of our babies, but Rose was the first of our grown children to go." He returned home for the funeral, then "left the newly made grave" to resume his organizing tour. He was, said a friend, "like a tugboat in the New York harbor. All machinery."

A year later, there was a near tragedy. He had arrived in Washington from New York early in the morning. He had an appointment with President McKinley, but had stopped briefly with his family. It was his custom to make his way around in Washington by bicycle. As he was leaving his home, a street-car hit him. He "never understood how," he said. Perhaps he was more tired than he realized. The force of the collision threw him about twenty feet. One of his bicycle wheels was smashed; a spoke punctured his right lung. He was carried back into his house, unconscious and with blood seeping from his mouth. Doctors found his ribs badly damaged and torn ligaments in his knees.

The accident came at a critical time. The Federation's convention was soon to open in Detroit, and Sam felt that his presence was urgently needed. He had been approached shortly before by lobbyists for a ship subsidy bill. They had offered him $10,000 for his support; he knew that they would be in Detroit seeking to buy support there. The Federation's membership had grown from 278,000 to 349,000 that year. There would be a number of new and untested delegates, he said, and he was uneasy about what might happen. But he was still confined to his bed when the convention opened, and reports from Detroit indicated that the lobbyists were busy there. At this point, a close friend wired Sam asking whether he could do anything for him. Sam wired back, "You are too far away." John Morrison was in Washington the next day. "You asked me if there was any way in which you could be of service," Sam told him. "There is. I do not think it safe for me to go to Detroit alone. I want you to go with me." Morrison insisted that Sam first get his doctor's advice. Sam agreed. The doctor ordered him to remain in bed. He went to Detroit anyway. Attended by Morrison, and using crutches, he hobbled into the convention hall, made his way to the platform, and told the story of the attempt to bribe him. "The men on that ship subsidy lobby are now in this hall," he said. "I could, if I wished, point to them where they sit. I am morally certain that they had made proposals to delegates to this convention." A vote on endorsement of the ship subsidy bill was taken immediately after he finished speaking. There was only one vote for it. As Sam was making his way painfully out of the hall, Max Hayes, a prominent Socialist, who frequently delighted in goading him, said: "Good for you, Sam." In mock dismay, Sam replied: "What have I said or done, Max, to win praise from you? It must be something awful." And he went back to bed for more than a week.

# 12

## *Critics: Left and Right*

Sam's influence in the Federation was often misunderstood. Many people assumed that his power was dictatorial; critics were fond of portraying him as the "boss" of the country's trade unions. This was absurdly inaccurate. His constitutional authority, as president of the Federation, was slight. The whole structure of the Federation had been designed by him and his associates, as he frequently explained, to prevent centralization of control. Its model had been the federal government. Sam's supremacy was real enough, but it arose from the force of his personality and ideas. The Federation convention's response to his dramatic appeal on the ship subsidy bill had demonstrated the special quality of his leadership once again. He earned the support of his associates, said one of them, "by his rectitude, courage, loyalty, and overwhelming wisdom."

Even if Sam had possessed the dictatorial power critics attributed to him, he would not have used it. The very concept of such power was hateful to him. He was a Jeffersonian democrat with an unshakable faith in the ability of free men to work together, in an orderly way, for the solutions to their problems. "I want to urge devotion to the fundamentals of human liberty," he told one AFL convention. "No lasting gain has ever come from compulsion. If we seek to force, we but tear apart that which united is invincible." He was a firm believer in what has come to be known as "participatory democracy." On a number of occasions, Senate committees asked him what could be done to "allay the causes of strikes." His reply was: "Nothing." He wanted politicians to "keep their hands off and thus to preserve voluntary institutions and leave the way open for individual and group initiative to deal with problems."

He carried this faith in voluntarism to an extreme that would now be regarded as archaic. He opposed compulsory social insurance. "Doing for people what they can and ought to do for themselves is a dangerous experiment," he wrote. He didn't want government to "interpose its authority and wisdom and assume the role of parent or guardian." He believed that it "lessened individual initiative." He argued that social insurance could not "remove or prevent poverty" because "it does not get at the cause of social injustice." It could only, in his view, "divide the people into two groups—those eligible for benefits and those considered capable to care for themselves." The only agency that attacked the root cause of poverty was the labor movement, he said. He advised "social busy-bodies and professional public morals experts to reflect upon the perils they rashly invite under this pretense of social welfare." He wanted legislation to secure for labor "the right to exert and exercise the normal human activities of self-development . . . freedom to fight and freedom to achieve." Nothing more.

Sam's forecast of "unparalleled" growth for the Federation was being glowingly confirmed. By 1902, it had more than a million members. Hundreds of organizers were in the field. In the one year, it had chartered 877 federal, or local, unions and 14 international unions. It was as if an immense logjam had been broken. Suddenly, workers were flooding into the Federation. It was still very far from being affluent, but it was no longer pinched for funds. Its income that year was $144,498. The 1902 convention raised Sam's annual salary to $3,000.

The Federation's growth had not silenced its radical critics. Many of them continued to ridicule it as "obsolete" or "petrified" and in less flattering terms. Sam himself was seldom free from harassment. Sometimes, mobs would disrupt his meetings and shout insults at him. Once, on leaving a meeting, he was followed by about fifty booing radicals. He lit his cigar and walked slowly toward his hotel. The mob howled. He walked more slowly. He would not give it the satisfaction of thinking that he was flustered. When a friend informed him that he was being attacked by Debs and others, he replied: "That is their business. I shall simply go on in my work as I see the light and duty." He bore "no ill will," he said, for "Mr. Debs and others who have never yet succeeded in any effort they have undertaken."

Within the Federation, Sam's critics sometimes tried to embarrass him on minor points in the hope that this would enable them to defeat him on major issues. A delegate complained at one convention that he and his wife had been kept awake by an alcoholic party in Sam's room. Sam never troubled to conceal the fact that he enjoyed a convivial evening. It was his way of relaxing after a hard day's work. But he was always alert for his duties the next morning. Moreover, his drinking companions could expect no special favors. "After a social hour" with Sam, said one union president, "you could not expect that he would deviate one iota from the straightforward business" at hand. The union president was rueful after one such occasion. Sam, he said, had "hardly recognized" him except in his official capacity. The president of the Federation was accused of frequenting a burlesque show in Washington; it was the one Justice Oliver Wendell Holmes was said to attend. At one convention, he was accused of smoking nonunion cigars; at another, he was charged with having been shaved

by a nonunion barber. Sam "confessed" to the last charge.
But, after dragging out his confession long enough to inspire a
sense of triumph in the breast of his critic, he announced that
the nonunion barber who had shaved him was "Sam Gompers."
The convention enjoyed the joke.

Many employers saw him as kin to the devil. A spokesman for
the National Association of Manufacturers (NAM) assailed the
"evil performance of the octopus known as the American Federation of Labor." "Our government cannot stand, nor its free
institutions endure, if the Gompers-Debs ideals of liberty and
freedom of speech are allowed to dominate," wrote David M.
Parry, president of the NAM. He denounced unions as "open,
organized rebellion" against the country's "institutions and
laws." The middle course, as Sam had learned early in his
career, doubled one's enemies. Their opposite views of him
provide an interesting example of how belief can distort reality.

The NAM philosophy at the time was based on a belief in
the semidivinity of capital, and 1902 heard a naked expression
of it from George F. Baer, a spokesman for the anthracite-
mine owners in Pennsylvania. "The rights and interests of the
laboring man," Baer said, "will be protected and cared for—
not by the labor agitators—but by the Christian men and women
to whom God, in his infinite wisdom, has given control of the
property interests of this country."

More than 140,000 miners were out on strike for higher
wages and against the raw injustices of company-owned towns
in which the coal companies exacted a kind of feudal tax on
everything from birth to death. The miners' average annual
earnings were estimated at $560. This was fairly good for the
time. However, the rent they had to pay in company-owned
shacks and the prices in company-owned stores and for other
company-provided services were exorbitant. Baer refused to
negotiate with the union. He refused even to meet with John
Mitchell, president of the United Mine Workers. The strike,
which had started in mid-May, dragged on. Sam had helped to

organize the bituminous coal mines five years earlier. He was thoroughly familiar with the situation and in constant consultation with Mitchell. He used all of his now considerable influence to bring pressure on the mine owners.

One means open to him was the National Civic Federation (NCF), an organization of prominent businessmen and trade unionists. It had been formed in 1900 for the purpose of easing tensions between labor and capital. Its chairman was Mark Hanna, the Republican boss who had managed President McKinley's campaign in 1896. He had since been elected a senator. The NCF managed to arrange conferences between the union and the mine owners, who were united in a trust called the Temple Iron Company, but these were unproductive. The NCF had suggested earlier that two prominent clergymen, Archbishop John C. Ireland, a Catholic, and Bishop Henry C. Potter, an Episcopalian, be asked to arbitrate the dispute. Baer rejected the proposal. "Anthracite mining is a business," he wrote, "and not a religious, sentimental, or academic proposition." Hanna, who had vast business interests of his own, required no instruction on the nature of business, but, though a conservative in politics, he accepted the idea that workers had rights.

Hanna once complained to Sam about a strike in his Buffalo blast furnaces. Sam told him that his foremen had been extorting "kickbacks" from the workers by threatening to discharge them. Hanna investigated, and found that this was so. "Sam," he said, "I didn't know that any such thing could exist in any plant and much less in a plant I owned." But, he added, "these men, in striking in blast furnaces, acted so undiplomatically." Sam's wry reply was: "That is true, Senator, very undiplomatic, but we don't raise diplomats on thirteen, fourteen, or fifteen cents an hour."

Baer, like Pullman, Frick, and other industrial autocrats of the period, had no patience with Hanna's acceptance of unions. Theodore Roosevelt had become President of the United States in 1901, when McKinley was assassinated by a young anarchist. In October, as the strike entered its fifth month, he grew concerned. The Congressional elections were approaching, and the country was facing a coal shortage. Senator Henry Cabot Lodge had asked: "Is there anything we can *appear* to do?" "I am at my wits' end how to proceed," Roosevelt said. Finally, he invited Mitchell and the mine owners to a conference at the White House. The country was threatened by a "winter coal famine," he said. He appealed to their patriotism. Mitchell was willing to submit the strike issues to arbitration. The idea repelled Baer. "We object," he told Roosevelt icily, "to being called here to meet a criminal even by the President of the United States." The President had no strong sympathy for labor; he was scornful of "popocracy." But he disliked being thwarted. He got word to J. P. Morgan, Baer's banker, that, if the mine owners persisted in rejecting arbitration, he would order the army to take over the mines. Morgan apparently intervened, and Baer decided to yield his mandate from God. Eventually, the miners got a 10 per cent wage increase, and many of the evils of the company-owned towns were eliminated. Sam, in his autobiography, called the strike the "most important single incident" in the history of the American labor movement. The unions had challenged the coal trust, and they had won.

Trusts were in bad repute at the time. Muckraking journalists had been exposing them for years, and Roosevelt had denounced the "malefactors of great wealth." There had been a meeting at Madison Square Garden to protest the refusal of the "coal barons" to arbitrate. The speakers had included Charles Francis Adams, whose father and grandfather had occupied the White House, and other men of prominence. At the end of the meeting, Sam had been approached by Arthur Brisbane, Hearst's brilliant columnist, who had $1,000 in cash from the publisher for the miners. Sam, wary in such matters, had Brisbane exchange the cash for a check made out to the miners.

The strike had been significant for another reason. Previously, Presidents had intervened in strikes only to break them. Roosevelt had acted to settle the miners' dispute. Sam, still skeptical of politicians, was nevertheless hopeful that a new day was dawning.

His attitude toward the National Civic Federation was equally a mixture of skepticism and hope. He had agreed to serve as a vice-president in the belief that it might be useful in "preventing hostile or inimical action." "The growing influence of labor," he wrote, "had convinced some employers" of the "wisdom of a policy of conciliation," but he entertained no illusions. "Peace on earth, good will toward men" was a hope not yet fulfilled.

The NCF, as could have been expected in the climate of the period, raised hackles on the necks of both conservatives and radicals. Neither believed that capital and labor could, or should, reconcile their differences. In the eyes of the National Association of Manufacturers, the NCF constituted "a great danger to the best interests of our common country." The radicals denounced it as an ingenious effort to dilute the militancy of labor, and Sam was accused of what to them was the dreadful crime of class collaboration. Much was made of the fact that he dined with employers at NCF dinners. The prevailing radical attitude was summed up in the saying "Feet that meet under mahogany tables don't kick." Sam regarded this attitude as childishly irresponsible. "In religion, I am a workingman," he wrote. "In politics, I am a workingman, and in every nerve, in every fiber, in every aspiration, I am on the side which will advance the interests of my fellow-workingmen." Unlike the radicals, however, he was not at war with capital. What he wanted for labor was an effective voice in deciding its conditions, and the improvements that would inevitably flow from it. Socialists, in and out of the Federation, picked at his slogan "More, more now." They wanted to know when, in his judgment, the "more" would be enough. His answer was that it would be unrealistic to set limits to labor's aspirations.

Sam was now a national figure. Newspapers quoted him eagerly. In the National Civic Federation and elsewhere, he was meeting with the country's industrial leaders. He was a frequent visitor to the White House; Roosevelt often wanted his help or advice. "Time and time again," Sam wrote, "Roosevelt had me at the White House from seven o'clock on—he with his tennis clothes on, and me without dinner." He was sought after as a lecturer at colleges and universities, and, when time permitted, he was happy to talk on the history and philosophy of the labor movement to young people who would have a large hand in shaping the future. In the colleges, as elsewhere, he was a popular speaker. He delivered a series of lectures at Cornell. There were four hundred students on the first day and fifteen hundred on the last. Sam's beard and mustache were gone; his hair had begun to recede at the temples; he wore wing collars; his shoulders bulged under a now well-cut coat. One imagines that he could easily have been mistaken for a senator or a college professor. But, in 1903, we find him speaking on "Labor's Rough but Noble Struggle," near Cumberland, Maryland, where posters announced him as "Labor's Foremost Champion." It was the only role that really mattered to him.

# 13

## *"Three Cheers for President Gompers"*

The defeat of Congressman Charles E. Littlefield, of Maine, would be a "positive calamity," President Roosevelt announced, weeks before the 1906 elections. The Republican Party had sent Secretary of War William Howard Taft, House Speaker Joseph Cannon, and Indiana senator Albert Beveridge into Littlefield's district to help him. It was said of Beveridge's oratory that one could waltz to it. There was reason for the Republicans' concern. The Federation was pledged to defeat Littlefield, who had consistently fought measures it favored. Sam had entered the campaign in mid-August. He had spoken at numerous meetings, one of them said to be the largest in Maine's history, and he was an effective campaigner. He struck at what he called Littlefield's connections with "corrupt corporations." He was aided by other labor leaders. As always, he enjoyed the battle. "The outlook is good," he wrote to an associate, "the big guns were here and thundering at me. The trusts and corporations have sent a quarter of [a] million dollars to buy the election if it can be done." It was revealed later that the National Association of Manufacturers had spent $60,000 in Little-field's campaign. It was not surprising that the Congressman, a Republican running in a strongly Republican district, was re-elected. But his margin of victory, which had been 5,419 two years earlier, was reduced to around 1,000. Sam was not un-happy.

His venture into Maine represented a change in his, and the Federation's, political policy. Early in 1906, he had told the Federation's Executive Council that there "seems to exist [in Congress] an utter disregard of either the interests, the re-quests, or the protests of labor." The outlook, he said, was "un-satisfactory and unpromising."

The Federation had a long list of grievances. Seamen had to make themselves liable to compulsory naval service as a con-dition of employment on privately owned ships. Workers often found themselves in competition with convict labor. Chinese were being brought into the country to compete with them. Americans were suffering from a severe case of Sinophobia. In St. Louis, Theodore Dreiser, then a newspaperman, noted that Chinese restaurants were nests for thieves. Henry George found Chinese "filthy in their habits." Sam's objection to them was based on economics. More than a dozen years earlier, Adolph Strasser, his old ally in the Cigarmakers' International Union, had complained that there were "only twenty-five cigarmakers left on the Pacific Coast . . . all the rest having been driven out by these imported coolies." "There is no antipathy on the part of American workmen to Chinese because of their nationality," Sam had said, "but to a people who menace the progress, the economic and social standing of the workers." "The Chinaman is a cheap man," he said on another occasion.

Later, in his autobiography, he sought to make amends. "It is my desire to state emphatically," he wrote, "that I have no prej-udice against the Chinese people. On the contrary, having some understanding of their history and the philosophy of their early sages, I have profound respect for the Chinese nation." Nevertheless, he believed that "the maintenance of the nation depended upon the maintenance of racial purity and strength." In a time of slavery, Thomas Jefferson and Andrew Jackson had owned slaves. Sam did not escape entirely from the influences of the society in which he lived.

But the competition of Chinese immigrants was one of the lesser concerns of the Federation in 1906. Its main grievance was that injunctions were being used to deny basic constitutional freedoms to workers and to cripple unions. It decided that a more active role in politics had become necessary. Its slogan "Reward Your Friends and Punish Your Enemies" soon sounded across the country. Sam, who had constantly downgraded politics in the past, was to find himself immersed in it until the end of his days. The fact is that, with the Federation's offices in Washington, Sam was spending more and more time with political leaders from the President on down. Possibly, he found it intriguing to be close to the centers of power.

After Littlefield's re-election, critics of the Federation said that its political influence was negligible. Champ Clark, a power in the House of Representatives, disagreed. He reported that Littlefield had had a large majority in a "standup" vote on one of his bills but that on a roll-call vote it was overwhelmingly defeated. "Why that remarkable and sudden shift in the minds of representatives?" he asked rhetorically. "President Gompers was against it—that's all."

But Sam's increasing influence made him a more tempting target. The fact that he couldn't be ignored meant to his enemies that he had to be compromised or beaten. One day, in 1907, he found a note in his mail that said: "You had better look out —the NAM is about to publish an exposé of labor graft in which you figure." It was signed "A friend." The NAM "exposé" did appear. It charged that Gompers had been receiving a "rake-off" on advertising in the AFL's monthly publication, *Federationist*. The NAM's source was an advertising solicitor who had been dismissed by the magazine for dishonesty; its charges were easily refuted.

A more elaborate scheme to embarrass Sam was hatched in the same year. He was visited one day by a man named Broughton Brandenberg, who said that he was an NAM specialist in exposing the immorality of union leaders. He told a bizarre story to the effect that Sam, when he was seriously ill in 1895, had signed a confession of immoral conduct. Sam knew that no such statement existed; he must have felt as if he were a character in a detective novel. However, he led his visitor on. Brandenberg offered to keep Sam's "confession" secret and "take care of him financially" if he would quit the Federation presidency after its convention. Sam listened gravely. He then reported the whole incident to members of his Executive Council. At the convention, where he again told the story, he received a roaring vote of confidence. A year earlier, Victor Berger, one of the Socialist leaders in the Federation, had been quoted as saying, "All of [the Federation's] proceedings are senile. Sam Gompers, the President and leading spirit, has more and more developed into an empty, self-complacent old fool." At the 1907 convention, Berger said: "For some years past, it has been my lot to come here and vote against the unanimous election of President Gompers. This year, I promised to move to make his election unanimous." He then called for "three cheers for President Gompers."

Brandenberg, it later turned out, was a thoroughly unsavory character. He passed forged checks and, after his arrest, jumped bail, but he wound up in prison.

Though the Brandenberg affair had all the earmarks of a detective story, the year also cast Sam in a drama of genuine significance. The Sherman Anti-Trust Act, passed in 1890, imposed triple damages for restraint of trade, and it had been invoked against unions when they struck or organized boycotts of nonunion products. In 1902, the Hatter's Union declared a strike and boycott against the Loewe Company, in Danbury,

Connecticut. The company promptly announced that all "members of labor unions, individually and collectively," would be held responsible for any damages it suffered. Subsequently, it claimed $240,000 in treble damages under the Sherman Anti-Trust Act. The case was to be in the courts for more than a dozen years, but, meanwhile, liens were placed on the homes and bank accounts of 240 workers, most of them well along in years.

In 1907, while the case of the Danbury Hatters was still pending, Sam himself became the principal character in another case. Workers at the Buck Stove and Range Company, in St. Louis, Missouri, had struck against the ten-hour day, and the *Federationist* had placed the company on its "We Don't Patronize" list. The company president, J. W. Van Cleave, was then president of the National Association of Manufacturers, and he saw this as a splendid opportunity to get at Sam. He obtained a sweeping injunction; it forbade even discussion of the strike. When the *Federationist* printed information about the strike, Sam, as its editor, and Frank Morrison, the Federation's secretary, who was in charge of circulation, were charged with contempt. Charges were also brought against John Mitchell, who had presented a resolution on the Buck Stove strike at the mine workers' union convention. In the District of Columbia Court, where the trial took place, the judge denounced them as "leaders of the rabble" who would "unlaw the land." They were, he said, "public enemies whose intent was to bring the relentless blight [of] anarchy and riot" down on the country. It was not really a shining example of judicial behavior.

Sam was given an opportunity to speak before sentence was imposed. It was an eloquent defense of the right to dissent.

> Freedom of speech and the freedom of press have not been granted to the people that they may say the things which please, and which are based upon accepted thought, but to say the things which displease, to say the things which may convey the new

and yet unexpected thoughts. . . . If men must suffer because they dare to speak for the masses of our country . . . if I cannot discuss grave problems, great questions in which the people of our country are interested . . . if speeches in furtherance of great principles are to be held against me, I shall not only have to but I shall be willing to bear the consequences.

Predictably, the judge was unmoved. Sam was sentenced to a year in jail; lesser sentences were imposed on the others. The sentences, however, were never served. Appeals were taken, and, in 1914, the sentences were set aside on a legal technicality. Meanwhile, Van Cleave had died; his successor had no desire to carry on his bitter crusade against unions. The basic issue of constitutional rights Sam had raised was ignored.

Nevertheless, Sam, as president of the Federation, had set the stage for the political battles that were to follow. In 1908, when the Federation representatives went to the Republican convention with an appeal for relief from injunctions, they were coldly ignored. The Democrats were more accommodating. Sam, in an open letter published less than a month before the election, asked all "lovers of human liberty" to support Bryan, who was again the Democratic candidate. Of labor's treatment by the Republicans, he wrote: "We asked for bread, and they showed us a whip."

Sam's relations with Roosevelt dated back to the 1880's when he had persuaded Roosevelt, then a New York State senator, to introduce a bill to curb tenement-house work. They had been friends and enemies a dozen times since then. Roosevelt often displayed a kind of small-boy arrogance. "Theodore," a fellow Republican had once said mockingly to him, "if there is one thing more than another for which I admire you, it is your original discovery of the Ten Commandments." Sam, on the other hand, could be immensely stubborn in defense of a principle, and he was no respecter of rank. He was "equally at ease," as he noted, with a ditchdigger and the President of the United States; it was not an attitude that endeared him to Roosevelt. In any event, Roosevelt now decided to snub Sam. He excluded him from a dinner party to which he invited other labor leaders. It was not Sam who was embarrassed. Unfortunately for the "Rough Rider," the other labor leaders, loyal to their "Chief," chose not to attend.

The Republican Presidential candidate in 1908 was William Howard Taft. Roosevelt had selected him with the idea that Taft, if elected, would pursue his policies. Taft, who weighed an incredible 354 pounds, was an outwardly meek man and intellectually timid. "What would you advise a man to do who is out of a job and whose family is starving because he can't get work?" someone asked him. "God knows," Taft replied. "Such a man has my deepest sympathy." He was also conservative. He thought that government could best be run "without injury to business" by lawyers "who understand corporate wealth." As a judge, he had issued one of the early injunctions against unions, and Sam campaigned against him as the "Father of Injunctions." Taft was elected, however, and in later years, meeting Sam, would say, "Hello, how are you, my old antagonist?" Sam eventually found Taft "one of the most genial and likeable men" he had ever met. But, as President, Taft, gave little comfort to labor. He vetoed a bill to end use of the Sherman Anti-Trust Act against unions as "class legislation of the most vicious sort."

In 1909, Sam had what is now called a "working vacation." The Federation's Executive Council had authorized him to attend several trade union meetings in Europe and to study the conditions of European labor. The council may have felt that, after his strenuous exertions in the campaign, he needed a rest. He sailed from New York—this time, he had first-class accommodations—on June 19, accompanied by an old friend, J. W. Sullivan. They visited England, France, Italy, and Austria-Hungary. One gathers from the account Sam wrote of it that the vacation was a happy one, but he found little to praise in European life. In Blackpool, England, he remarked that the teen-agers "were the smallest people in stature" he had ever seen in an English-speak-

Gompers greets members of his family and childhood
friends, during a visit to England, where he lived until
he was ten years old. (AFL-CIO *News*)

ing community. "Not only was the average height hardly more
than five feet; but narrow, bony shoulders, span-width chests,
and spindle legs were the rule." It was the result, he suggested,
of generations of child labor. In Amsterdam, he asked a man who
was weaving cane bottoms for chairs how much he earned.
"Forty cents a day," he was told. "What would it buy?" he
asked. "Bread and potatoes" was the answer. "Earnings of less
than four cents an hour in a day of five-thousand-dollar auto-
mobiles were grotesque," Sam thought. In Budapest, he was
appalled to find women working as hod-carriers and being paid

"about as much for a week's work as a New York hod-carrier earns in a day." But, in Germany, where strong trade unions had raised the standard of living, he found that "large numbers of working-men" were becoming "among the best-looking of Germany's people." "The distinctive type of drudge" was disappearing in Germany, he thought. But his vacation wasn't spent entirely in investigating labor conditions. He found Paris splendid and Rome, which he was seeing for the first time, fascinating.

Nevertheless, when he returned in mid-October, he said that European travel made revolutionists of all Americans. "They revolt against the almost general antipathy to plain water and pure air," he wrote, "against the universal tipping system, against the European theatre, and against the colossal blunder, from start to finish, of the European railroad."

In every respect, he had found Europe inferior to America. Our education system was better. "We have done with kings and czars and nobles. Our heroes are men and women." And: "Our people do not stand under the dreaded shadow of war, which is the case constantly in the countries having large standing armies, with aristocracies of officers associated with the classes to whom war might be financially or politically profitable."

# 14

## The McNamara Case

Ever since Bryan's campaign in 1896, there had been a steady weakening of the control exercised by financial interests in the federal government and in the country generally. The Senate was no longer, as it once had been, a "millionaire's club." The number of "insurgents" in the House of Representatives was growing. The muckraking journalists had turned public opinion against the trusts. The Federation, which had a million and a half members by 1909, had become a center of the reform movement. Sam, when he was in Washington, was frequently approached by congressmen in rebellion against the autocratic rule of the House of Representatives. The autocrat was Joseph Gurney Cannon, of Illinois, a Republican and Speaker of the House. Sometimes referred to as "foul-mouthed Joe" because of his lurid language, he had been in Congress since 1873. Using the Ways and Means, Rules, and Judiciary committees, which he controlled, he exercised a nearly absolute rule over the House. Cannon was hostile to all labor and reform legislation, and Sam had campaigned against him in 1908. In Danville, Illinois, he had

116

noticed that nearly everything, from the "Cannon Brothers' Bank" to "Cannon's Whiskey, 8 Years Old," seemed to be owned by the Speaker. It symbolized for Sam the alliance between wealth and those in political power. He denounced Cannon as the "Mephistopheles of American politics," a label cartoonists and editorial writers were happy to pick up. If it hurt Cannon politically, the election results failed to reveal it.

Sam continued to battle him. In 1909, nineteen insurgent Republicans met with Sam in the Federation office to plan Cannon's overthrow. All but three of them were from Western states where there was now a radical tradition among the farmers. George William Norris, of Nebraska, was among them; he was to emerge as one of the country's great progressive leaders. When the fight came in the House, Cannon tried to get the support of Tammany Democrats. Norris shamed them. "Hold up your manacled, wounded, bleeding, shackled hands," he thundered, "and let the country see your parliamentary slavery."

But that was a while later. Meanwhile, Sam had again found himself beleaguered. On October 1, 1910, an explosion wrecked the *Los Angeles Times* building and killed twenty-one people. The owner of the *Times*, General Harrison Grey Otis, had long been a bitter enemy of labor. Sam, in St. Louis the day of the explosion, expressed shock. There had been a good deal of violence in labor disputes. "I deeply hope," he told a reporter from the *St. Louis Star*, "that no one who was connected with the labor movement will be found to have done it." "Labor," he said, "does not stand for such outrages, nor contemplate such crime. . . . It was the act of a madman." But the *Times* charged that it had been the work of someone connected with labor. Sometime later, William J. Burns, of the Burns Detective Agency, kidnapped John J. McNamara, an officer of the Bridge and Structural Iron Workers, in Indianapolis, and brought him to Los Angeles, where he and his brother, J. B. McNamara, had already been indicted for the crime. There was some evidence that the explosion had been caused by gas. The fact that the Burns

Agency, like the Pinkerton, had been involved in numerous
efforts to break unions, persuaded most labor people that it was
a frame-up. The McNamara case was a sensation all across the
country. Sam knew John J. McNamara as a "devoted, practicing
Catholic." He had never met the other McNamara. Both men
pleaded innocent. The Federation raised money for their defense; Clarence Darrow was hired as their counsel. Sam visited
the McNamaras in the Los Angeles jail. John J., grasping Sam's

In a Los Angeles jail, Gompers visits James B. (left) and John J. Mc-
Namara, who had been indicted for blowing up the *Los Angeles Times*
building. (AFL-CIO *News*)

hand, said: "I want to assure you that we are innocent of the crime with which we are charged." As the case approached trial, Darrow became pessimistic. He was disturbed by the inadequacy of the funds available to him. "I am simply not going to kill myself with this case, and then worry over money and not know what to do," he wrote. There were other complications. Lincoln Steffens, who had "muckraked" politics and who had now become interested in labor, thought that, if the McNamaras confessed, they could be used somehow to persuade labor and capital to accept the Golden Rule. Steffens saw himself as a radical and Sam as "a crooked old labor boss." "I and my sort," he told William J. Burns, are "more down on Sam than you are. "Oh, hell, yes," Burns replied, according to Steffens. "Fellows like you . . . are always about 1,000 years ahead of all of us." Steffens had long sessions with the McNamaras. There are conflicting accounts of what actually happened. But, on December 1, while Sam was in a train from Washington to New York, two newspaper reporters approached him with the news that the McNamaras had pleaded guilty. He told a friend that he was "shocked and astounded" by the McNamaras' "confession of the terrible crime." He also felt betrayed. He had put the prestige of the Federation behind them. The Federation for him, it was said, was "the Father, Son, and Holy Ghost." At Pennsylvania Station, in New York, he walked into a swarm of reporters and detectives. If the McNamaras had pleaded guilty, he told them, he had no "alternative or desire than to believe them guilty."

But reporters and detectives hounded him for days. There were persistent efforts to link him to the crime. Burns announced almost daily that he would "get the man higher up." Sam's innocence was doubted. The *Wall Street Journal* said sardonically, "Mr. Gompers seems almost too good to be true. He has managed to reach the highest position in labor politics while preserving a pristine innocence of mind beside which a new-born babe seems wallowing in original sin. . . . The innocence of Mr. Gompers is a source of public danger." Newspapers demanded

Sam's resignation. Interviewed by New York reporters, he said: "The whole business makes me sick."

The McNamara case came to a sorry end on December 15, 1911. J. B. was imprisoned for life; John J. received a fifteen-year sentence, which was later reduced for good behavior. At the Federation convention in 1921, John J. approached Sam and pleaded not "to be condemned in the eyes of labor for evermore." "If you had told me that you were guilty, I would not have betrayed you, and you know it," Sam replied coldly. "You should never have risked the prestige of the entire labor movement." John J. offered his hand; Sam ignored it.

Before the McNamara case had reached its climax, Sam himself became the victim of a frame-up. He had spoken in Oakland, California, on Labor Day, from a table draped with an American flag. A photograph retouched to show him standing *on* the flag was widely used. He proved that the photograph had been faked, but it was damaging just the same. Answers seldom catch up with accusations.

Attacks on Sam and the Federation seemed to be pouring in from all quarters. Charles William Eliot, who had recently retired as president of Harvard, published a book, *The Future of Trade Unionism and Capitalism in a Democracy*, in which he strongly criticized many of the techniques, including the boycott, unions considered essential to their success. Sam didn't believe in allowing such criticism to go unanswered. His reply was rude but telling. Eliot's book, he wrote, suggests a

> comfortable, stall-fed, old bossy cow imparting her pious ruminations to a listening group of well-housed, tender, and meek-eyed veals: Nothing serious is wrong with this world, children. Green pastures are within reach of all. So, be good. Don't horn one another. That's naughty. Take the feed your kind masters give you. And, above all, never refer to the butcher. It's a very unpleasant subject, butchering; forget it.

# 15

## A Buoyant Time

Not everyone turned against Sam as a result of the McNamara case. He had answered some criticism by Roosevelt; Roosevelt had replied: "It is a real pleasure to receive an article written in such a moderate and gentlemanly tone, after the experience I have had with what I can only call the scurrilous black-guardism of Harrison Grey Otis." Possibly, Roosevelt was thinking ahead to the 1912 elections and hoped for the support, or at least the neutrality, of the Federation's president.

The party nominating conventions were to disappoint both of them. At the Republican convention, the Taft forces bested Roosevelt after a furious battle; Roosevelt, unwilling to accept defeat, became the candidate of Progressive, or "Bull Moose," Republicans. Sam, who worked for the nomination of Champ Clark, a congressman friendly to labor, at the Democratic convention was "much disheartened" when the convention chose Woodrow Wilson, president of Princeton University.

It has been said that Sam distrusted Wilson because Wilson was a professor. Perhaps. But Wilson's writings suggested conservative leanings. Some conservative Democrats had put him forward as a possible opponent to Bryan in 1908. It would be

an excellent thing, Wilson had written, if a way could somehow be found to "knock Bryan into a cocked hat."

Sam didn't allow his disappointment at Champ Clark's defeat to weigh on him. The Federation's membership was now
more than a million and a half. In 1910, the Democrats had
captured control of Congress. He had come to identify labor's
interests with them. Labor's own political influence was soar-
ing. "We have curbed the sordid, self-seeking agents of pre-
datory interests," he had told the Federation convention in
1910. Labor-supported candidates had been victorious in California, New York, Wisconsin, Maine, and a half-dozen other
states. In several states, there had been victories for the direct
election of the judiciary and for direct primaries and direct election of senators and for other political reforms labor had been
advocating. Fifteen trade unionists had been elected to Congress in 1910. The following year, Sam was able to report that
W. B. Wilson, a member of the United Mine Workers' Union,
had become chairman of the House Labor Committee and
that the committee included three other trade unionists. Charles
E. Littlefield, his target in the 1906 congressional campaign in
Maine, had resigned. "The sentiment against him" that labor
had created, Sam said, "was too strong to withstand." "We are
no longer journeying in the wilderness," he told the convention. "We are no longer in the season of mere planting and
hoping. We are in the harvest time."

Wilson, who was elected in 1912, immediately gave Sam
additional reason for optimism. "The working people of
America," Wilson said, "are the backbone of the nation." Then,
in a direct reference to Taft's message vetoing anti-injunction
legislation, he said, "No law that gives [workers] freedom to
act in their own interests [can] properly be called class legislation or anything but a measure taken in the interests of the
whole people." The country's new President went further in
pleasing Sam and his fellow unionists. He appointed W. B.
Wilson his Secretary of Labor. Sam was delighted. He would
soon regard President Wilson with almost "reverential awe."

Gompers and his wife, Sophia, whom he called "Mother Gompers." She quietly accepted the hardships his life as a pioneer labor leader imposed. (AFL-CIO *News*)

Then, Congress passed, and Wilson signed, the Clayton Act. Presumably, it outlawed the use of injunctions in labor disputes. In 1891, at Logansport, Indiana, Sam had said, "You cannot weigh a human soul in the same scales with a piece of pork. You cannot weigh the heart and soul of a child with the same scales upon which you weigh a commodity." The Clayton Act, which declared that "the labor of a human being is not a commodity or an article of commerce," seemed to echo his words. He hailed it as "labor's Magna Charta." He was overly optimistic. Corporation lawyers and the courts would still manage to hamstring labor. For a time, however, it seemed that labor's long-sought political objective had been achieved.

In 1908, the Federation convention had authorized the building of a national headquarters in Washington. It was finally completed in 1916. Sam's son Henry, the Federation's first office boy, had become a granite-cutter. He had asked permission to contribute the cornerstone. The inscription had been written by Sam. It read: "This edifice erected in the cause of Labor, Justice, Freedom, Humanity." The dedication ceremony, which was attended by President Wilson and the Secretary of Labor, gave Sam an immense sense of achievement. It reminded him of "the old days when the morning of a labor gathering found travel-stained labor men sleeping on benches in the railroad station." He had led the Federation, with an interruption of only one year, since 1886. It had begun life in a shed on East Eighth Street, in Manhattan, with boxes for chairs, tomato crates for files, and only $160.52 in its treasury. It had had no status and a background of labor failures. Few people had expected anything of it. But here it was, in its own building in the nation's capital, with President Wilson and a host of other notables in attendance, a membership grown to more than two million, a power in the country. It was a "proud day" for him, Sam said. He "gave orders that each morning the American flag should be raised on our flagpole and under it the pennant of the A.F. of L." The order, he said, typified his conception of the relationship of the Federation to the United States.

Sam was a patriot. Even at the worst moments in his life, during depressions or periods of severe oppression, he had never faltered in his conviction that this was a land of hope. In 1893, Lucien Sanial, a leader of the Socialist Labor Party, had denounced the United States at an International Labor Congress in Brussels. Sam had thought it "akin to treason" to "befoul an adopted country." He had resented what he called "the misrepresentation of the spirit of America." It was one of the things that divided him from the more extreme radicals. He had not allowed hardship or injustice to turn him against the country. He had always been able to see, in pragmatism and courage, the promise of progress.

But he had as little use for jingoists as he had for the country's detractors. He had spoken out against them during, and following, the Spanish-American War. He had done so again in 1912 when some Americans had tried to provoke intervention in Mexico. Díaz, a dictator, had been overthrown. Unions had begun to blossom. Some American investors had been worried about what might happen to their Mexican holdings. "We are utterly opposed to any intervention in Mexico," the Federation had declared. "We believe in a determined policy of 'hands off.' We extend our cordial greetings and best wishes to the men in Mexico now struggling to abolish age-old wrongs."

But tension had continued. For a time, the Hearst newspapers had run an American flag at the top of their editorial pages, with the slogan "Plant It in Mexico and Never Take It Down." The *Los Angeles Times* had been another leader in the effort to provoke American intervention. In 1916, the situation reached a climax. The bandit Pancho Villa had conducted border raids. General "Black Jack" Pershing had been sent into Mexico on a punitive expedition. He never found Villa, and some American soldiers were taken prisoner by the Mexican authorities. Wilson demanded their release. Venustiano Carranza, the President of Mexico, ignored him. War between the two countries seemed imminent. In an effort to head off the crisis, Mexican labor leaders had been invited to meet with the Federation's Executive Council. Sam now wired Carranza:

> In the name of common justice and humanity, in the interests of better understanding between the peoples and governments of the United States and Mexico, for the purpose of giving the opportunity to maintain peace and avoid the horrors of war, I appeal to you to release the American soldiers.

Carranza immediately replied that his government had ordered "the liberty of the American soldiers." The crisis dissolved.

Now, the country was again in a Presidential campaign. This time, Sam worked vigorously for Wilson's re-election. The Republican candidate was Supreme Court Justice Charles Evans

Hughes. Sam attacked him as having "concurred in the decision which had mulcted 240 aged hatters, not one of them under seventy years of age, in the sum of $300,000. "The courts had finally decided against the Danbury Hatters. Labor had denounced this as a "Shylock decision." Roosevelt, back in the Republican Party, accused Wilson of "playing second fiddle to Gompers" in the Mexican situation. Sam recalled that Roosevelt had frequently had him in the White House "to consult on various matters." He was in the center of events. It was a buoyant time. Earlier in the same year, Senator Lawrence Y. Sherman, of Illinois, against whom he had campaigned, had called him a "public nuisance." "The most fortunate thing that has ever happened to Mr. Gompers," he had said in the Senate, is that he "escaped indictment" in the McNamara case. "Gird up your loins, Mr. Gompers," he had challenged, "and answer me like a man." Sam had promptly challenged him to a debate. The Senator had declined. Claude Bowers, a young journalist who was to gain distinction as a historian and as American Ambassador to Spain, and who admired Sam, thought that the Senator had been discreet. "After the debate," he wrote, "Sherman would have been in the belly of the fat man of the Federation."

Sam, in his sixty-sixth year, had developed a paunch. Comedians could extract a laugh from audiences by patting their "Gompers." His name had become a household word. More than that, his influence in the country had been acknowledged by the highest possible authority. After the elections that year, he had had a call from a White House staff member. To him, "more than any other one man," he had been told, "was due the re-election of President Wilson." "The common people have stood the test and have proven true," Sam had wired the President. "The cause of labor, justice, freedom, and American patriotism, and humanity has been vindicated."

Actually, that cause was being severely challenged.

# 16

## *Wartime Episodes*

Wilson had been re-elected on the basis of the slogan "He Kept Us Out of War." The war had been raging in Europe since 1914. It had become increasingly unlikely that the United States would remain on the sidelines. Then, on February 1, 1917, Germany declared unrestricted submarine warfare and began to sink American ships on their way to England and France. Sam cabled an appeal to Carl Legien, president of the German Federation of Labor. "Can't you prevail upon German Government," he asked, "to avert break with the United States and thereby avert universal conflict?" Legien replied that the British blockade was starving "our women, children, and aged." He appealed to American workers "not to allow themselves to be made cat's-paws of war-mongers by sailing the war zones." Sam cabled a second appeal to him. It was useless.

Sam had, in effect, taken his stand at the outbreak of war in 1914. The Carnegie Peace Foundation had been preparing to publish a volume of his articles and speeches on peace. He had withdrawn the manuscript. His dreams of world peace had been "ruthlessly destroyed," he wrote. He was "no longer a pacifist."

American labor was now involved in the country's preparedness drive. Sam was making speeches to unite the diverse national groups in the labor movement behind Wilson's leadership. Wilson named him to the Advisory Commission to the National Council of Defense. Labor had been accepted into the American family.

The American flag went up first on the Federation flagpole, but Sam didn't forget the importance of the Federation pennant immediately below it. "We speak for millions of Americans," said a declaration by a labor conference in Washington. "We represent the part of the nation closest to the fundamentals of life. We maintain that it is the fundamental step in preparedness for the nation to set its own house in order and to establish at home justice in relations between men."

In November 1917, President Wilson echoed this sentiment at the Federation convention in Buffalo. "While we are fighting for freedom," he declared, "we must see, among other things, that labor is free." It was another proud day for Sam. Never before had a President of the United States appeared at a labor convention. Sam introduced him as a "man of destiny." Wilson praised Sam's "large vision and patriotic courage."

Sam's annual salary had been raised to $7,500, and the Gompers had acquired their own home in Washington. It gratified an "intense desire" he had had "since childhood to have a home with four separate walls that were not attached to anyone else's walls," he wrote. "I wanted a real house surrounded by trees and grounds where flowers could grow and where I could watch the birds and hear them sing." At sixty-seven, the dream of the slum-reared boy had been fulfilled. He was to have little time to enjoy it.

When the Gompers family moved into their new home, the country was at war. The man who had devoted his life, not to an abstract humanity, but to "living, breathing men and women" inevitably found himself emotionally involved with those who were serving in the army. He felt a "deep personal concern for all active participants," one of his granddaughters recalled some years ago. "He never missed a chance to visit the camps here to talk with the men, and he saw as much as possible of our troops abroad, both in the trenches and in base hospitals, during a tour while the war was going on." Apparently he was well received. He believed that the soldiers knew, he said, that he was doing all that was "physically and humanly possible to aid for victory, and that I had their personal welfare at heart." But he found the hospital scenes depressing. They were "horrible," he wrote. In Dunkirk, he narrowly escaped becoming a casualty himself. A shell from a German Big Bertha tore an immense hole in a road fifty yards ahead of the car in which he was traveling.

In Britain, at the beginning of the war, unions, in a patriotic fervor, had agreed to waive labor standards on war production. As a result, workers had become exhausted by long hours; production had suffered. Sam, although revolted by "the atrocities and arrogance" of the Kaiser's armies, wasn't carried away by his emotions. He worked strenuously to maintain standards. He was willing to subordinate labor's interests to the national interest, but he was stoutly unwilling to have them sacrificed.

In 1917, in Bisbee, Arizona, armed vigilantes rounded up 1,186 striking Phelps Dodge workers and deported them to a desert town in New Mexico. The Arizona State Federation of Labor sent a curt wire to President Wilson asking: "Are we to assume that Phelps Dodge interests are superior to principles of democracy?" Wilson was hurt. The attitude of the union men in Arizona, he complained to Sam, was "unjust and offensive." Yes, Sam agreed, the telegram was unkind. But he suggested that Wilson "take into account" the Arizona unionists' "indignant resentment" at what they had suffered at the hands of "capitalist anarchists." The President was powerless to intervene in the dispute, but he ordered the military to care for the deported men.

During the war, as could have been expected, patriotism became an excuse for all kinds of ugly excesses. In the Northwest and in other areas, the Industrial Workers of the World, popularly known as the "Wobblies," came under attack from Loyalty Leagues and other such groups of superpatriots. Sam had little love for the IWW. It had been formed in 1905 as a rival to the Federation. It had brought together Debs, DeLeon, and a colorful mixture of other socialists and anarchists and syndicalists. Its constitution denounced the Federation's conservatism. It wanted to root out capitalism. It believed in "direct action" —violence and sabotage—and it had been involved in a number of spectacular strikes and free-speech fights. It appealed mainly to miners, loggers, and migrant workers. "Halleluiah, I'm a Bum" was its favorite song. Its leader, William Dudley ("Big Bill") Haywood, a massive, brawling idealist, regularly denounced Sam and his associates as "labor fakers." Sam shrugged off all this.

He told Newton Baker, Wilson's Secretary of War, that the constitutional rights of the IWW could not be "denied by any citizen or group of citizens under a free government by law. Denial of liberty and rights," he wrote, "are not the methods by which abuses of liberty and rights will be corrected." As for the disruption of production being caused by the IWW, he advised Baker that "the only effective action that the government can take is to remedy the fundamental wrongs" the IWW was protesting.

"We have little, if any, sympathy with the expressions of those who are opposed to our system of government," he had told a Federation convention years earlier. "We may be their outspoken antagonists. But we should at all times maintain the constitutional rights of the people of free speech and free assemblage." Even in the midst of war, he wanted those rights upheld.

# 17

# *A Very Lonely Man*

By the summer of 1918, the Allied powers were in difficulty. A great German offensive had been turned back in the second battle of the Marne, but people were wearying of the bloodshed and the terrible hardships war had imposed. Peace propaganda was sapping their morale. Two main sources of this propaganda were Germany, which had a network of agents everywhere in Europe, and the Bolsheviks, who had seized power in Russia the previous November and had negotiated a separate peace with the Germans. In addition, there were those in every country who saw the war as simply another expression of imperialist rivalry. Sam had received "urgent" invitations from England, France, and other Allied countries. He was wanted, as the leader of American labor, to speak against a negotiated peace that would leave the German army in control of areas it had conquered. It was said in Europe that President Wilson and he were the only Americans the European people trusted. Wilson asked him to go.

On August 16, he sailed from New York on the *Missanabie*;

it was part of a fourteen-ship convoy carrying forty thousand American soldiers. German submarines were prowling the sea lanes, and portholes and doors had to be closed at dusk to prevent any light from showing. Few people ever enjoyed crossing an ocean in what Hemingway called the "vomitstink" of a troop transport. Sam, who had celebrated his sixty-eighth birthday at the beginning of the year, found the August heat "oppressive" as the convoy zigzagged its way across the Atlantic. At night, he couldn't even venture out on deck for one of his cherished cigars. A day and a half out of Liverpool, which was their destination, a submarine scare halted the convoy. For a while, as Sam watched, curious as ever, the escorting destroyers scurried about nervously. Then, the voyage was resumed.

On August 28, he stepped ashore at Liverpool to be greeted by representatives of British labor and the American and British governments. The War Department, which was in charge of arrangements, had barred reporters. As the car in which Sam was riding pulled away from the dock, he saw the reporters, several of whom he recognized, standing in the street. He told his driver to stop; he emerged from the car and chatted for a while with the reporters. He had long made it a policy not to neglect them. Besides, he had a statement he wished to make. The American Labor Mission, he said (he was accompanied by three other Federation officials and his secretary, Guy Oyster), was in England, and would go to France and Italy, "to aid in strengthening the bonds of unity so that we may all stand behind our respective democratic governments to win the war for justice, freedom, and democracy." It was to be his constant refrain. He wanted, he said to "rally men in defense of what makes life worth while."

In London, at an Inter-Allied Labor Conference, he met the peace-at-any-price advocates head-on. They wanted to meet with labor representatives from the Central Powers to talk peace. Sam was willing to meet with those who were "in open revolt against their autocratic rulers." There were acrid ex-

changes. Finally, the Federation program, which followed
President Wilson's famous Fourteen Points, was adopted. Sam
was accused of running a "steam-roller" over the conference.
"If five Americans," he replied, "could put their program
through a meeting of over seventy-four delegates . . . we were
entitled to the victory won."

Some respected historians now argue that a negotiated peace
would have been desirable. This may well be. But hypotheses
about history are always easier to manage than the realities.

The London *Times* hailed Sam as a "robust democrat." Lloyd
George, Britain's wartime Prime Minister, said that Sam stood,
with Roosevelt and Wilson, as one of the three great men the
United States had produced during his (the Prime Minister's)
lifetime. Ray Stannard Baker, an American journalist, saw Sam

> striding down [a London street], a powerful, squat figure fol-
> lowed, a step behind, by a looming bodyguard of labor leaders.
> He was scattering the assembled and gaping subjects of King
> George, however well inured to the sight of potentates, to the
> right and left. His hat was set well back on his head, his chin was
> thrust forward, and he was throwing aside humorous remarks to
> his followers. So I saw him once again in Paris. So he strode full
> fronted throughout Europe, so sure of himself and his entire
> equipment of ideas, so conscious of the immense power of
> American labor behind him, that he scattered to the right and
> left all peoples of all nations. He told British, French, and
> Italian labor leaders, quite positively, what they must do to be
> saved.

In the United States, Sam had become something very close
to a folk hero. It was nearly impossible for him to walk into a
hotel lobby or a railroad station, or to appear in a street, without being recognized and greeted as "Brother Gompers" or by
his first name. A friend, who received a telegram from him
while on a train, suddenly found the trainmen wonderfully
solicitous. Any friend of Sam's, apparently, was entitled to spe-

cial treatment. Sam encountered the same recognition and warmth wherever he went in England and on the Continent. American soldiers, in army camps, at base hospitals, and at the front, which he toured, greeted his arrival with cheers and requests that he speak. The Europeans were equally friendly. He was received by kings, prime ministers, admirals, and generals. In Paris, his old friend, Paul Deschanel, now President of the Chamber of Deputies, invited him to speak to that body. He received a rousing ovation. One day, while he was in Paris, it was reported that some German spokesman had described American soldiers as "the most bellicose" they were facing.

Gompers with Sophia and his daughter Sadie in 1915. (AFL-CIO *News*)

"Did they expect to have a pink tea with us as invited guests?" Sam asked an audience.

It had been planned that his tour would end in Turin, Italy. He had just concluded a speech there when John P. Frey, one of his associates, told him that he must return to his hotel at once. Sam, thinking that it was some new task, rebelled. He had been driving himself hard for months. He wanted a few hours of relaxation. Frey insisted. At the hotel, Sam was told to "brace up to receive a piece of bad news that will go to your very soul." His only remaining daughter, Sadie, had died in the "flu" epidemic.

Sadie had been his favorite. She had been the only child still living with her parents, and it had been one of Sam's delights at home to listen to her sing. Months later, in Washington, one of Sam's granddaughters, Florence Gompers McKay, was present when he opened a trunk containing gifts he had bought in Europe for Sadie. Sophia was with him. Both of them wept broken-heartedly as each gift was removed from the trunk. Possibly, a sense of guilt compounded his sorrow. He seemed never to be present when tragedy struck his family. He had been in Des Moines when Rose had died, and he had been away on other disastrous occasions. Friends said that Sadie's death was a blow from which he never recovered. The effect on Sophia was more evident. "Mother," Sam wrote of his wife, "never came back to herself after our Sadie's death." A close friend of the Gomperses' saw Sophia "dressed in black, bent and listless. It was obvious," she wrote, "that the will to live had been crushed in her."

Shortly after Sadie's funeral, which had been delayed until his arrival, Sam was again off on his travels. He went first to Chicago for a conference of union leaders on war problems, then to Laredo, Texas, for a conference to establish a Pan-American Federation of Labor. He had been pushing toward this objective since 1912. He envisioned a federated organization of democratic unions reaching down across the continent.

He was in Laredo, on November 11, about to address a rally when a reporter handed him a "flimsy" containing the terms of the armistice ending the war. Sam was exultant. But he knew that his own war would continue. The following month, in New York City, he was addressing a meeting of union leaders. "I am sixty-eight years of age," he said. Fatigue showed in his face. The skin under his eyes had gone slack and was deeply creased, and, under his chin, it was strangely mottled. Except for a few tufts of gray, his hair was gone. He looked old. But his head, which gave the appearance of having been chiseled out of granite, and the line of his mouth still suggested the indomitable character that had carried him through so many battles. "He had a great square head, like a Rodin sculpture," an artist wrote, "ragged and ugly, tremendous and elemental." "I have been tried and seared as few men have," Sam continued. "I have had almost my very soul burned in the trials of life." But he was not prepared to retire. "Somehow or other," he said, "I believe that there are considerable years of fight in me for labor."

But now disaster seemed to stalk him. In 1919, he went to the Versailles peace conference. He was instrumental there in setting up the International Labor Organization. He was called back to meet a growing labor crisis in the United States: A steel strike was threatening. There were other alarms.

He was riding in a taxi in New York when it collided with another car. He suffered several broken ribs and other internal injuries. For a week, he would permit no one to see him. Then, he summoned a friend, Lucy Robins, with whom he was working for an amnesty for Eugene Debs and others who had been imprisoned for their opposition to the war. "I want no one to know but you," he said in an even voice. "I am going blind. The doctors say it is temporary, a result of the accident. I know better." She chided him for being "morbid." "I didn't expect any moth-eaten consolation from you," he replied. "I want help. I want you to be near me whenever you can."

The following year, there was another blow. Sophia died.
They had been married for fifty-three years. She had never
complained about hardships, she had raised their children, and
she had provided a warm atmosphere in their home. Daniel J.
Tobin, a member of the Federation's Executive Council and
one of Sam's close friends, had been present once when Sam
was playing with his father, who was then over ninety and
blind. "The father was guessing whose hands were over his
eyes," Tobin wrote. "After several guesses, he finally said: 'It's
my boy, Sammy.' (The 'boy, Sammy,' was then about 70.) The
human picture of that family and the love and reverence each
of them had for one another impressed me greatly." Until
Sadie's death, there home had been a happy place. "He liked to
gather his friends in it," wrote one of his granddaughters, "and
enjoy an evening of music (he had one of the early Victor
phonographs and a splendid collection of records), a game of
cards or just good conversation." The Gomperses had held open
house on Sunday when Sam was in Washington; union leaders,
political leaders, educators, clergymen, actors, and musicians
would gather there. "They were all welcome" to Sam, said his
granddaughter. "He liked them all; he liked to entertain them
in his home." The deaths of Sadie and Sophia ended this chap-
ter in his life. "My home family had been taken away from
me," he wrote. "I was left a very lonely man."

The thought of living alone was too much for him. He re-
married. His second wife was thirty years his junior, and she
had little sympathy with his ideals. One gathers that she had
been dazzled by his high position in American society. The
marriage was a disastrous arrangement for both of them. Sam,
pain-ridden as a result of his accident, harassed by domestic
difficulties, and nearly blind, must have felt that fate was pushing him hard. He was too busy to complain. "The work of the
labor movement does not grow less, for it has its roots in vital
needs," he wrote. "There are such wonderful possibilities in
the life of each man and woman." He hoped to keep on with
his work until he went out "into the silence."

An artist described the AFL president as having a "great square head, like a Rodin sculpture, ragged and ugly, tremendous and elemental." (AFL-CIO *News*)

# 18

## *The Inevitable Day*

"Socialists have always called me blind," Sam remarked sourly to a friend. "What a field day they would have if they knew the truth." Only those closest to him were aware of his fading vision. Aided by his staff, which was enormously devoted to him, he swept into the turbulence of postwar America as if he were a man at the height of his powers.

William Allen White, the journalist, observed Sam closely during the industrial conference called by President Wilson in October, 1919, in Washington. The purpose of the conference was to conciliate the differences between labor and industry. Many of the country's industrialists had reverted to the auto-cratic attitudes of the prewar period. Workers were restless. More than 4 million were to go out on strike before the year was over. As the conference met, a strike in the steel industry, which involved more than 300,000 workers, was in its third week. Workers in steel mills were still on a twelve-hour day. Investigators for the Federation of Churches had found the wages of unskilled workers "inhuman." Strikers in the steel

towns were being ridden down by the Coal and Iron Police.
They were being denied the right to meet. Elbert H. Gary,
chairman of the mammoth U.S. Steel Corporation had refused
to negotiate with the unions. Gary was at the conference as a
"public representative." Sam headed the labor representatives.

White watched Sam, "the most interesting figure in the conference," as he arraigned Gary for conditions in the steel industry and for his refusal to negotiate with the unions. "His
face was mobile," White wrote, "his mouth was large and
strong, his jaw was brutal and indomitable. He had the big
nose of a ruler; but his eyes—there was mystery! They were
sheathed in thin saurian lids; when he opened them wide, they
gave a flaming effect to his face." The journalist hadn't noticed.

White thought that Sam was "carrying the conference with
him," but the employers balked at the idea that workers had
the right to be represented by unions. "Are we," Sam had
challenged, "in this year of grace 1919, having driven political
autocracy from the face of the globe to submit servilely to an
industrial autocrat?" President Wilson's conference, as far as
Sam was concerned, had failed. He led his labor delegation out.

Weeks earlier, Sam had walked into a meeting of the Boston
Chamber of Commerce to denounce the city's Commissioner of
Police. The Boston police force had struck. It was not an action of which Sam approved. Indeed, he had discouraged the
chartering of police unions. But the Boston strike had been
used deliberately to discredit trade unions. The Police Commissioner had failed to call out his volunteer force, and had, in
effect, abandoned the city to criminals and rioters. Sam's recita-
tion of the facts had little, if any, influence. President Wilson,
on a speaking tour to gain popular support for the League of Nations, paused in Helena, Montana, to denounce the strike as a
"crime against civilization."

New and painful problems seemed to be mushrooming up
all around Sam. The war had been followed by a wave of anti-
Communist hysteria. A characteristic newspaper cartoon of

1919 showed a Communist, armed with a dagger labeled "Bol-shevism" and a torch labeled "anarchy," crawling out from be-hind an American flag. The FBI was arresting hundreds of radicals in raids all across the country. "There is no time to waste on hair-splitting over the infringement of liberty," said the *Washington Post*. Socialists who had been elected to the New York State Legislature were refused their seats. "Socialism is Bolshevism with a shave," said the *Detroit Journal*. Unions, too, were under attack as being under Communist control.

Some local unions had succumbed to Communist influence. The Seattle Central Labor Council endorsed the Soviet regime, and sent a delegate to the Third International, which the Bol-sheviks had set up to organize world revolution. The Federa-tion itself, however, had been among the first to condemn the Bolshevik dictatorship.

Sam had welcomed the first Russian Revolution, in which the Czar was overthrown. He had detested the Czarist regime as he detested all autocratic government. Thirty years earlier, the Federation had opposed an extradition treaty then being negotiated between the United States and Russia. The treaty, Sam had said, would mean that our government would "deliver to the Czar and his hangman" every Russian patriot "seeking to liberate the Russian people from the yoke of despotism." He had argued passionately that this country "must forever remain the asylum for all who dare to brave danger for freedom's sake." In the spring of 1917, when the Czar was deposed, Sam was elated. "We rejoice with the Russian workers in their newly achieved liberty," he cabled the Russian Duma. "International labor welcomes the triumph of freedom and the downfall of despotism throughout the world." The Bolshevik revolution was another matter.

It had been hailed by many people as "the dawn of a new day for humanity." Lincoln Steffens, on returning from a visit to Russia, announced: "I have seen the future and it works." But Sam was not beguiled by the drama of the revolution or by

the humanitarian pronouncements of its leaders. He saw behind the rosy haze to the grim facts. Freedom of speech, press,
and assembly, granted by the first revolution, had been abolished
by the Bolsheviks. The right of workers to organize had been
similarly abolished. As he saw it, this made the whole idea of
Bolshevism "outcast in the minds of civilized men." "We shall
progress by the machinery of democracy," he declared, "or we
shall not progress. There is no group of men on earth fit to
dictate to the rest of the world."

A meeting was arranged between Sam and a visiting Soviet
commissar. Lenin had ridiculed the American Federation as a
"rope of sand." "Tell Lenin," said Sam, "that our 'rope of
sand' will prove stronger than his iron chains." He was told
that the suppression of civil liberties was essential to the success of the revolution. "Have we been fighting czarism all these
years," Sam asked, "just for a change of chains?"

In an article in *McClure's Magazine*, in 1919, he wrote,
"Those who see wisely into the future must, if society is to be
saved from fires more consuming than those we have known,
so shape the course of the world as to offer this hideous wrath
of destruction no foothold." Few people then saw the reality as
clearly; it did not improve his standing with the American left.
Under Sam's leadership, the Federation became one of the
first organizations to enter the struggle against Communism. It
was not until the Hitler-Stalin pact that many people were to
understand what Sam had understood more than a generation
earlier.

However much he was opposed to Communism, Sam refused to yield to the anti-Red hysteria. In 1886, in the midst of
similar hysteria, he had pleaded for clemency for the anarchists arrested after the Haymarket bombing. "I abhor injustice,"
he had said then. The years had not altered him. In 1917, Lucy
Robins, a young radical, had come to Sam's office to solicit his
help for the movement to free Tom Mooney. Mooney had
been convicted of throwing a bomb into a preparedness parade

in San Francisco and had been sentenced to death. It was widely believed that he had been framed. Sam's secretary had turned Miss Robins away. She had sent him a note saying, "I now understand why the great masses of workers despise you, curse you, and eagerly await your death." A message from him overtook her as she was about to board a train for New York. He wanted to see her. In his office, he said, laughing, "Suppose I should die? What would you do? If you have any good ideas, I might be willing to cooperate." He then asked one of his secretaries to produce the Mooney file—"all of it." It revealed that he had been in the thick of the movement to "free Tom Mooney" from the beginning, and that most of the victories for which the radicals claimed credit had, in fact, been engineered by him.

Now, heedless of the consequences, he was working for an amnesty for all those who had been imprisoned for their political opposition to the war. They included the Socialist leader Eugene Victor Debs; "Big Bill" Haywood, the leader of the IWW; and the anarchists Emma Goldman and Alexander Berkman. Most of these people had been his bitter enemies. Let them "come out and condemn me," he said. "It is their personal right." He believed that "every man must have his liberty, and that right should be protected above everything else."

The *New York Times* disapproved. It wondered why "Mr. Gompers . . . a sound and active American patriot [was] pleading and working for the benefit of those who, whether as so-called conscientious objectors or as unconscientious seditionists and disloyalists, did all they could to defeat the United States in the war." The editors apparently could not understand his concern for justice.

Neither could President Wilson. He refused Sam's persistent appeals that he grant an amnesty. "The professor of history," Sam commented, "has lost his historical perspective."

Wilson was having his own tragic difficulties. The country had turned against his concept of a "peace without victory."

"The American people want Germany smashed," Roosevelt had roared. For the Republicans, the moment had come to defeat what they saw as the Wilsonian movement toward socialism. Participation in the League of Nations was never approved by the Senate. Wilson, exhausted by his efforts to win popular support for the League, had broken down. He was bedridden for the four years of life that remained to him.

The ranks of Lloyd George's triumvirate of great Americans had been thinned: Roosevelt had died in his sleep at his Oyster Bay home; Wilson, paralyzed by a stroke, was waiting

Gompers is shown here with Robert LaFollette, during LaFollette's campaign for the Presidency of the United States in 1924. (AFL-CIO *News*)

Gompers' first plane trip took him to Rochester, New York. He had missed his train. (*The American Federationist*)

for death; Sam, older than the others, was driving forward to his destiny. A diabetic condition was added to his other afflictions. He had to follow a rigid diet. It offended him. He could never understand restrictions of any kind. In May, 1924, he was in Lenox Hill Hospital in New York. He had collapsed. The Federation's Executive Council voted to pay his medical bills. He refused. Members of the Executive Council argued that they wanted to "preserve for the labor movement the inestimable value of his services." He would have none of it.

He had resumed his duties on leaving the hospital. It was

obvious that his energy had been depleted, but he had no desire
to spare himself. The Democratic and Republican conventions
had turned a cold shoulder to labor. There was a third candidate, however. Robert M. LaFollette, with whom Sam had
worked in the fight to depose "foul-mouthed" Joe Cannon,
had become the candidate of a newly formed Progressive
Party. "[I] made up my mind," Sam said, to put the last bit of
energy I have into the campaign for LaFollette." One day,
while in New York, he was informed that LaFollette was in
the city and planned "to visit his sick friend, Sam Gompers."
"I'll go to him." Sam said, "and that will show everyone that I
support him." They met at the Waldorf-Astoria. LaFollette,
taking Sam's hand, said, "This is the man I wish to serve." Sam
would not be outdone: "I have come to salute President La-
Follette," he said.

LaFollette polled nearly 5 million votes, more than any third-
party candidate had received in American political history, but
Calvin Coolidge, who had risen to prominence by crushing
the Boston police strike, was elected.

We catch a glimpse of Sam now leaving Washington for
the Federation convention in El Paso. He is accompanied by
his eldest son, Sam; his son's daughter, Florence; and her daughter. Sam walks down the length of the platform, clasping the
hand of his great granddaughter. She is wearing a red beret. He
refers to her as his "little Red Cap." It is to be his last visit with
his family.

At El Paso, it was sensed that the grand old man of American
labor was nearing the end of his run. His mind was still wonderfully keen, but he seemed to have shrunk physically. His opening speech, which was read for him, suggested a last testament.
He spoke as the "only delegate" who had participated in labor's
deliberations since the Federation of Organized Trades and
Labor Unions met in Pittsburgh in 1881. The democratic process, he said, "may seem a cumbrous, slow method to the im-

patient, but the impatient are more concerned for immediate triumph than for constructive development."

The convention was a reverential tribute to him. The International Ladies' Garment Workers' Union, which he had helped to organize at the beginning of the century, presented a bust of him. The delegates rose to their feet and applauded. A reporter wrote, "Mr. Gompers, not knowing what it was about, began looking around him. He rose slowly to discover the source of the excitement, and collapsed into his chair . . . tears rolling down his cheeks." His acknowledgment left the audience in tears. "It was more than a tribute to a great leader," the reporter wrote. "It was a brooding upon the inevitable day when he would be no more."

After the convention, at which he was re-elected by a unanimous vote, he and other Federation leaders went to Mexico City for the inauguration of President Calles. Sam, who had worked valiantly for a democratic Mexico, was a hero to the Mexicans. In Mexico City, he stood on the balcony of the presidential palace with Calles and his predecessor, Obregón. The Mexicans were tall men. Sam, standing behind them, was not at first visible to the throng, estimated at one hundred thousand, in the square below. Calles drew him forward. Sam, with his instinctive sense for the dramatic, stepped between Calles and Obregón and raised their hands in his. "*Viva* Gompers!" the crowd roared, "*Viva* Gompers!"

The next day, while his associates watched with mounting anxiety, he was at the congress of the Pan-American Federation of Labor. But his vitality, once so prodigious, was gone. With President Calles' personal physician in attendance, he was rushed to San Antonio. It was hoped that the lower altitude would help. "Go at once," doctors had told members of his party. In San Antonio, doctors administered epinephrin to stimulate his heart, and he was bled to relieve congestion in his lungs. The treatment proved futile. On December 13, at 2:30

A.M., his nurse heard him whisper, "Nurse, this is the end. God bless our American institutions. May they grow better day by day." These were his last words. Less than two hours later, he was dead.

An old woodsman's saying tells us that it is difficult to judge the length of a tree until it has been felled. As the black-draped train carrying Gompers's body moved across the country from San Antonio to Washington, D.C., where he was to lie in state in the Presidential Room of the Union Station, tens of thousands gathered along the way and thronged into the stations for a final glimpse of him. There were high government officers, trade union officers, some of whom had known Sam for almost half a century, and anonymous men and women, many of them accompanied by their children, in the crowds. "Not since the days of Lincoln's last journey," wrote one observer, "had there been such a continent-wide outpouring of human sympathy and love." Newspapers from coast to coast carried the story on their front pages. The *New York Times* headline said: "SAMUEL GOMPERS DIES IN SAN ANTONIO, BLESSING 'OUR GREAT INSTITUTIONS'; NATION MOURNS GREAT LABOR CHIEF."

In the White House, President Coolidge, one of Sam's numerous adversaries, commented, "Mr. Gompers' whole life was devoted to the interests of organized labor until his name became almost synonymous with the cause he represented." There were tributes that would have pleased Sam more. In San Francisco, a construction worker knelt in prayer on a girder at the fortieth story of a new skyscraper. In Lawrence, Massachusetts, a family placed a bust of Sam on its front lawn. The inscription read, "Samuel Gompers: Labor's Champion, Humanity's Friend."

He had died a poor man. It was said that he had left only a "few thousand dollars." But historian Mary Beard, in summing up his career, wrote that he had left a "great estate built by decades of tireless endeavor." The estate was, she said, "a giant machine" and program that have "withstood the batteries of radical fire . . . a machine with a mind operating American fashion."

The vision the chunky, swaggering little cigarmaker had brought to the labor movement as a young man had been transformed into an enduring reality. It would remain for others to seek more distant horizons.

# Chronology

1850   (January 27) Samuel Gompers born.
1860   At age of 10, he leaves school to help support his family.
1863   Unable to earn a living in London, his father, a cigarmaker, brings family to New York.
1864   Sam joins cigarmakers' union.
1866   After working at home with his father, he gets his first factory job.
1867   Marries Sophia Julian who worked in cigar factory with him.
1873   Meets Ferdinand Laurrell, a major influence in his life.
1875   Elected president of Cigarmakers' Local 144.
1877   Leads cigarmakers' strike, and is blacklisted when strike is lost.
1881   Helps to found Federation of Organized Trades and Labor Unions of United States and Canada.
1886   American Federation of Labor is organized, and Sam is elected president.
1894   Defeated as AFL president.
1895   Re-elected.

1897  Defies injunction denying West Virginia miners right of free speech and assembly. It is beginning of his long fight against injunctions as judicial tyranny.

1898  Criticizes imperialist mood in country following Spanish-American war.

1906  Leads AFL into political action.

1907  Efforts made to "frame" him.

1908  Sentenced to year in jail for violating injunction.

1910  Defends McNamara brothers against dynamiting charge, and becomes target of press attacks.

1914  Hails Clayton Act, signed by President Wilson, as "labor's Magna Charta" in expectation that it will end use of injunctions in labor disputes.

1916  Helps to avert war between United States and Canada. Appointed to Advisory Commission to Council of National Defense.

1918  Takes lead in establishing Pan-American Federation of Labor. Heads American labor mission to Europe.

1919  Suffers severe injuries in accident, becoming partially blind.

1920  Wife, Sophia, dies.

1924  (December 13) He collapses in Mexico, is rushed back to San Antonio, Texas, where medical treatment proves unavailing, and he dies.

# Suggestions for Further Reading

Samuel Gompers' two-volume autobiography, *Seventy Years of Life and Labor*, completed just before he died, provides interesting and valuable insights into the early labor movement in this country. Mary Beard's *A Short History of the American Labor Movement* is an excellent and sufficiently detailed review for those who want to know more about the subject. Two other books a reader will find rewarding are *Samuel Gompers: Champion of the Toiling Masses* by Rowland Hill Harvey and *The AFL in the Time of Gompers* by Philip Taft. Finally, *Tomorrow Is Beautiful* by Lucy Robins Lang is a highly personal account of how Gompers and the labor movement appeared to a militant young radical of the period.

153

# Index

Garland, Hamlin, 70
Gary, Elbert H., 140
Gary, Joseph E., 55
George, Henry, 43, 53–54, 108
German Federation of Labor, 127
*Gilded Age, The* (Twain and Warner), 27
Goldman, Emma, 143
Gompers, Rose, 96
Gompers, Sadie, 135
Gompers, Samuel J., 25, 26
Gompers, Sara, 14
Gompers, Solomon, 14, 138
Gompers, Sophia, 25, 135, 137
Gomperz, Emric, 14
Grange, 47
Grant, Ulysses S., 88
Greeley, Horace, 16, 91
Greenbackers, 46

Hand-in-Hand Society, 40, 91
Hanna, Mark, 76, 95, 103
*Harper's Weekly*, 37, 90
Hatter's Union, 110–11
Hay, John, 38, 53, 95
Hayes, Max, 98
Hayes, Rutherford B., 37, 38
Haymarket bombing, 142
Haymarket Square, 54
Haywood, William Dudley, 130, 143
Hearst press, 125
Henry George Legions, 54
Hillquit, Morris, 73, 74
Hillquit-Gompers exchange, 73–74
Hirsch, David, and Company, 30–31
Homer, Winslow, 44
Homestead Act (*1862*), 26
"Homestead Day," 67
House Labor Committee, 122
House of Morgan, 44
Hughes, Charles Evans, 125–26
Huntington, Collis, 27

Industrial Workers of the World, 130
Inter-Allied Labor Conference, 132
International Labor Congress, Brussels, 124
International Labor Organization, 136
International Ladies Garment Workers' Union, 147

International Typographical Union, 58
International Workingmen's Association, 24, 29, 66
International Workingmen's Congress, 66
Ireland, John C., 103

Jackson, Andrew, 109
Jefferson, Thomas, 19, 109
Julian, Sophia, *see* Gompers, Sophia

Kirchner, John, 67

LaFollette, Robert M., 146
LaSalle, 31
Laurrell, Karl Malcolm Ferdinand, 31–32, 41–42, 47
League of Nations, 144
Legien, Carl, 127
Lenin, V. I., 142
Lennon, John B., 85
Leslie, Frank, 63
Liebknecht, Karl, 66
Lincoln, Abraham, 23
Littlefield, Charles E., 107–8, 109, 122
Lloyd George, David, 133, 144
Lodge, Henry Cabot, 104
Loewe Company, 110–11
London *Times*, 133
*Los Angeles Times*, 117, 125
Loyalty Leagues, 130

McBride, John T., 79–81, 84–85
*McClure's Magazine*, 142
McGregor, Hugh, 66
McGuire, Peter J., 22, 29, 51, 83–84
McKay, Florence Gompers, 135
McKinley, 95
McNamara, J. B., 117–18, 120
McNamara, John J., 117, 120
McNamara case, 116–20
Madison Square Garden meeting (*1893*), 72
Marcuse, Herbert, 81
Marx, Karl, 24, 30, 31
Marxian socialists, 46
Melville, Herman, 21
Mitchell, John, 102, 111
*Moby Dick* (Melville), 21
Mooney, Tom, 142–43

Van Cleave, J. W., 111
Vanderbilt, Cornelius, 21
Versailles, 136
Villa, Pancho, 125
*Volcano* (Tom-ri-John), 29

*Wall Street Journal*, 119
War Department, 132
Warner, Charles Dudley, 27
*Washington Post*, 141
Weaver, James B., 89, 91
Western Federation of Miners, 94
Western Labor Union, 94

White, William Allen, 95, 139, 140
Whitman, Walt, 45
Wilson, W. B., 122
Wilson, Woodrow, 14, 121–22, 124, 126, 127, 128, 129, 131, 133, 140, 143–44
"Wobblies," *see* Industrial Workers of the World
Woodhull, Tennie C., 29–30
Woodhull, Victoria, 29–30
*Woodhull and Claflin's Weekly* (T. and V. Woodhull), 29
World War I, 127–36